HUDSON STEA____

by

Graham Atkinson

*Above : A dramatic view of the **Hudson Venture** on 5 June 1971 when she was about to enter service.*

(Company archives)

*Front cover : It is the bridge-amidships colliers which will come to mind for many readers when they reflect on the fleet of Hudson Steamship. There is a good supply of monochrome photographs of these ships but good colour photographs are much more difficult to find. With hatch covers open ready for discharge, the 1949-built **Hudson River** heads up the Thames on 8 August 1971.*

(World Ship Photo Library)

*Back cover : Just over a decade later, the changed appearance of an east coast collier is evident in this view of the 1977-built **Warden Point** passing South Shields and heading up the River Tyne on 14 August 1981.*

(World Ship Photo Library)

INTRODUCTION

Coal was the dominant fuel of the Industrial Revolution. It powered Britain and the world. Coal from northern England and South Wales was shipped all over the world and the fortunes that it made for individuals gave it the nickname black diamonds.

The powerhouse of the British Empire was London and coal was needed to satisfy the voracious appetite for both domestic and industrial consumers. For centuries collier brigs had sailed from the north-east of England and eastern Scotland to London and the south-east. With the Industrial Revolution demand grew and the advent of the steam engine saw fleets like Cory, Stephenson Clarke and France Fenwick emerge.

In the mid-1800s Charles Hudson opened an office at Hartlepool as a coal factor, or agent. Coal was originally carried from the colliery on the backs of donkeys to the beached brigs. In time coaling staithes were built and railway lines ran from the pithead to the staithes and the coal was tipped into the ships' holds. Charles Hudson's business expanded and he opened offices in Sunderland, Newcastle and then London. Soon after his London office was opened, Hudson died and his business was acquired by Samuel Williams. Williams had long been associated with Dagenham Dock on the Thames and it was here that coal was discharged for distribution to his customers in London's East End.

The Great War saw heavy shipping losses which caused a shortage of ships available for charter and so Williams, first through John Hudson & Co Ltd and then Hudson Steamship Co Ltd, entered ship owning in his own right. A small fleet was built up to serve Dagenham and other customers and the business survived the industrial depression of the 1920s and 1930s. In World War 2, however, the collier fleets as a whole now faced aircraft, mines and E-boats following the fall of France as Hitler tried to bring about Britain's surrender. Many ships and their crews were lost as the steam colliers endeavoured to keep London supplied with coal.

Following World War 2, the incoming Labour Government implemented a policy of nationalisation which included the power industry. A nationalised collier fleet now competed with the private operators who set about replacing their war losses. Hudson looked to other cargoes for its modern fleet and entered the West Indies bulk sugar trade. Consequently the company ordered its first motor ship specifically for worldwide trading and during the 1950s tried to reduce its dependency on the north-east coal trade, although demand would pick up during the winter months.

In the 1960s, one of the company's ships was used in trials which resulted in a new generation of motor colliers being built for Hudson, Stephenson Clarke, France Fenwick and Cory. The 1960s also saw the company dispose of its postwar built steamships in favour of deepsea motor ships, built through partnerships with Scandinavian owners, and it entered the supertanker trade.

Following the takeover of the Williams Hudson group, Hudson Steamship Co Ltd saw its fortunes wane until it was sold to the Norwegian ship owner Hilmar Reksten. Coinciding, ironically, with an upturn in the north-east coal trade in the early 1980s, the number of vessels managed by Hudson increased. In 1989 Hudson was sold to the Norwegian ship owner Mosvold and it was through this company that it enjoyed a renaissance in ship management. Through subsidies from the Norwegian government, cargo ships and bulk carriers were bought secondhand by Mosvolds, as market forces allowed, and placed under Hudson management.

Sadly because of events elsewhere within the Mosvold group, coupled with a shift in trading and owning patterns to the Far East, the fleet declined. Eventually Hudson was put up for sale and with no buyer closed down in 1996.

When I began my research into Hudson Steamship in the early 1980s, the company was still in existence as a ship owner although it was a minor player in what was left of the north-east coal trade. Nevertheless it had survived while others had gone to the wall although by the end of the decade it was no longer involved in the trade but was still in shipping as managers for deep sea ships.

Graham Atkinson

Blyth, October 2004

Published by Bernard McCall, 400 Nore Road, Portishead, Bristol, BS20 8EZ, England. Website : www.coastalshipping.co.uk
Telephone/fax : 01275 846178. E-mail : bernard@coastalshipping.co.uk
All distribution enquiries should be addressed to the publisher.

Printed by Amadeus Press, Ezra House, West 26 Business Park, Cleckheaton, West Yorkshire, BD19 4TQ
Telephone : 01274 863210; fax : 01274 863211; e-mail : info@amadeuspress.co.uk; website : www.amadeuspress.co.uk

ISBN : 1-902953-14-2

GENESIS : WILLIAMS & DAGENHAM

John Hudson & Co Ltd became shipowners in 1915 with the building of their first ship. Prior to this the company business had been as coal agents for coal shipped from the coalfields of Northumberland, Durham and eastern Scotland to the Thames using chartered ships. However, as a result of war losses to shipping during World War 1, which led to a shortage of suitable tonnage, the company decided to become owners in its own right.

The company origins can be traced back to the 1840s when a coal exporting partnership, Mesnard and Hudson, was formed in Hartlepool, County Durham. Its offices were given as Town Wall. John Hudson was a skilled linguist and acted as Consul for Sweden, Norway, Russia and several German states. Even before the partnership was formed the Hudson family were involved in the shipment of coal. In the 18th century it was common practice for the collier brigs to be beached and coal brought to them at low water on the backs of donkeys that had carried it from the colliery.

In the late 1850s an office was opened at Sunderland by which time the company had been restyled John Hudson & Co. They traded as coal exporters and timber merchants as well as ship and insurance brokers. John Hudson lived at 29 Norfolk Street, Sunderland and the offices were initially in the Exchange Buildings, but eventually moved to 62 John Street where they remained until the turn of the century when they moved down the road to 16 John Street. For a time John Hudson's private residence was also at 62 John Street. He moved to 4 Mowbray Terrace about 1885. The Sunderland office was agent for the Bearpark Coal & Coke Co for over thirty years and also represented the Earl of Durham's colliery interests until they were disposed of to Lord Joicey.

In 1881 the company opened offices in Newcastle at 2 Lombard Street, trading as coal factors. The offices were moved in 1889 to 17 King Street. John Hudson died in the early 1890s and his son, Charles Hudson, born in 1851, took over the business until his death on 26 May 1904.

In 1901 Charles Hudson formed a new company, John Hudson & Co (London) Ltd, to purchase the Thames business of Hudson, Pearson & Fernie, formed in 1899. The new company had a capital of £50,000, Charles Hudson being the Governing Director, holding 8,510 out of 8,516 issued shares. Following his death Frank Marshall and Alfred Benjamin Wilkie of Newcastle were appointed directors of the company.

A controlling interest in John Hudson & Co (London) Ltd was purchased by Samuel Williams & Sons Ltd, which owned Dagenham Dock, one of the many wharves handling coal on the Thames. Originally wharfingers and lightermen Samuel Williams & Sons Ltd had entered the bunker trade to meet the demand of the increasing number of steamships using the Thames. As a result they came into contact with John Hudson & Co (London) Ltd. In September 1904 two of Samuel Williams & Sons' directors, William Varco Williams and Frank Williams, were appointed to Hudson's board. On 25 May 1909 the company was restyled John Hudson & Co Ltd. In 1915 John Hudson & Co Ltd created a subsidiary company, John Hudson (Tyne & Wear) Ltd, based in its offices in Newcastle and Sunderland.

Samuel Williams had been born in 1824, his family originally coming from Gloucestershire. At an early age Samuel and his parents moved to Christchurch, Surrey. On 13 May 1841 Samuel was apprenticed for seven years as a lighterman to Charles Shutton of St Mary's, Lambeth. After finishing his apprenticeship he probably worked as a journeyman and in 1855 began his own lighterage business, Samuel Williams & Sons, rafting timber from ships to timber ponds. He also bought ice from Norway, storing it in an underground ice store and selling it to fish merchants in the summer months. He did not have an office, working as did other lightermen, from a mooring on the river front and carrying out business from public houses.

Had it not been for his wife Elizabeth the company might never have been founded. Samuel Williams had an adventurous nature and aspired to being a mountaineer and Arctic explorer. His wife obviously succeeded in dissuading him from these notions. Their marriage resulted in the birth of seven children. The two eldest were daughters, Annie and Emily, followed by William Varco, Samuel, Frank, Alfred and Arthur. Samuel Williams' entry into business was backed financially by a Cornishman from St Austell called Varco. It is possible this person was Thomas Varcoe, Varcoe and Varco being two of several spellings of the surname. Thomas Varcoe inherited a large sum of money and properties from his father John Varcoe who died in 1852. In 1865 Thomas Varcoe entered shipowning as a part owner in the sailing ship *Eclat*. Another partner was John Varcoe, an accountant who was possibly his son. Thomas Varcoe died in 1885, aged 84, while his son John had died the previous year aged 58. Samuel Williams obviously held his financial backer in high esteem as he christened his eldest son William Varco Williams, and asked Varco(e) to be the child's godfather.

Samuel Williams purchased his first steam tug in 1861. Named *Little Eastern* she had been launched in January 1858 at Greenwich, the same month Brunel's *Great Eastern* had entered the water at Millwall. Her name is thought to reflect that occasion. She was under Williams' ownership for four years before being sold, by which time he had another two larger tugs and had begun to own dredgers for use on the River Thames.

On 23 March 1863 Williams secured a ninety nine year lease from Battersea Park Commissioners for a piece of land with a river frontage of 120 feet immediately upstream of Albert Bridge. This was to meet the expansion of his fleet of river craft and gave him a base where he could repair and build barges. In September 1865 he expanded the site, acquiring a further frontage of 137 feet from the Commissioners. With the change from sail to steam, Williams had in 1855 opened a coal bunkering depot in the Victoria Dock, the year the dock opened.

Another diversion for Williams was the carriage of tar, creosote and ammoniacal liquor from gasworks. These substances, by-products of the gasworks, were previously transported in barges fitted with tanks. Williams proposed decking over a barge's hold and making the hold into a tank. He secured a sixty year contract with Beckton gas works and a fleet of forty tanker barges was constructed. The barges were owned until the contract expired in 1936, although many were sold off from 1924 onwards. In 1884 he patented a dredging ladder capable of dredging to a depth of sixty feet yet still able to be fitted to a small hulled vessel.

Samuel Williams took his sons William Varco and Frank into partnership in July 1886 and the following year they purchased the land around Dagenham Dock, which had been the site of several failed attempts at development. The land was bought from the mortgagees of the Dagenham (Thames) Dock Co which had recently been wound up having failed to find finance for the development. Williams was able to fill in the marsh with spoil from the tunnels being dug for the London Underground system. His barges and tugs were being used to transport the spoil for dumping at sea. Instead the spoil was tipped into the marsh. Two piers were built in 1888 and 1889 to handle the spoil as the existing pier was not suitable. By 1894 an area of about thirty acres had been filled to the level of the sea wall which surrounded the marsh and had stood twelve feet above the level of the marsh before work commenced. What is more remarkable is that every barge load of spoil had to be shovelled into buckets and hoisted into tipping wagons by steam crane as there were no grab cranes available at that time. Also by 1894 the east and west piers had been completed and these exclusively handled spoil, while No 1 jetty handled coal. Colliers could be discharged at any state of the tide using four thirty hundredweight hydraulic cranes and buckets. A 1,500 ton cargo could be discharged in approximately fourteen hours.

On 31 December 1897, Samuel Williams & Sons Ltd was incorporated with a capital of £230,000 in £100 shares (500 preference and 1,800 ordinary). The company was formed to purchase the business of Samuel Williams & Sons, as of 1 January 1898. The business was given as lightermen, dredging contractors, coal merchants, coal factors, chemical manufacturers, colliery owners and wharfingers. Samuel Williams was made Governing and Life Director, while William Varco, Frank, Alfred and Arthur Edward all became Life Directors. Throughout its lifespan the company's shareholding would remain completely within the Williams family.

The assets transferred to the new company included premises at Princes Wharf, near Battersea Park, and the Dagenham Dock Estate. River craft included four steam dredgers, eight steam tugs, 134 open barges and 42 tank barges, three sailing barges, sundry small craft and *Britomart*. Share transfers included 2,237 ordinary £5 shares and 1,970 'A' Preference £5 and 'B' Preference £5 shares. Also included were £7,978 10s 0d Perpetual Debenture Stock and £13,478 10s 0d. Debentures in Deep Navigation Collieries Ltd, a 8/64 share in the steamship *Northumbria* and a further ten £100 shares and ten £1,000 debentures in the Rea Steamship Co Ltd.

The initial shareholders in Samuel Williams & Sons Ltd were:

Samuel Williams	300 Preference plus	500 Ordinary shares
William Varco Williams	50	299
Frank Williams	50	300
Alfred Williams	50	300
Arthur Edward Williams	50	300
Elizabeth Ann Williams		100
Hubert Edward Williams		1

Two years later, on 28 August 1899, Samuel Williams died. Varco Williams succeeded his father as Chairman, looking after commercial affairs in London, while his brother Frank, a qualified engineer, was based in Dagenham and responsible for engineering developments. The company's capital was increased in October 1900 to £280,000 with the issue of five hundred £100 Preference shares.

The 1890s saw further development at Dagenham. Larger cranes were installed on the jetties and larger barges built. Shortly before Samuel Williams death the company decided to spend £50,000 on a fleet of new barges and tugs as well as a new jetty with electric grabbing cranes and generating plant. In 1900 the dredger *Gleaner* was delivered, the dredgers by this date being operated by a syndicate, Ballast Dredger Owners Ltd, of which Varco Williams was Chairman. In 1914 the Port of London Authority assumed responsibility for river dredging and two years later the company ceased all its dredging activities.

The new coaling jetty completed in 1903 was built entirely of reinforced concrete. A new kind of crane was designed for this No 4 jetty to discharge colliers. Though hydraulic cranes had no superior in terms of ease and smoothness of operation they were vulnerable to frost damage, as had been shown in the winter of 1895 when the Thames had frozen over. Four cranes each weighing forty tons were built, powered by electricity, and each using a three ton grab. Power was generated in a power house built near the jetty. These cranes remained in service until 1939. On 18 December 1906, Samuel Williams & Sons Ltd was placed in voluntary liquidation, replaced by Samuel Williams (1906) Ltd. The company's title was changed back to Samuel Williams & Sons Ltd in 1907.

In 1911 **HMS Thunderer** was launched by the Thames Ironworks. She was the last and largest warship to be built on the Thames. Such was her size it was agreed she would be fitted out at Dagenham and a new concrete jetty was completed in nine months for that purpose, along with workshops on shore. In March 1912 **HMS Thunderer** sailed from the Thames, the cost of building her proved too great for her builders and they went into liquidation. Samuel Williams & Sons acquired some of the workshops and permission from the Port of London Authority to use the quay, officially known as No 5 Jetty but nicknamed "The Thunderer".

In 1923 the last of the debentures issued in 1906 were liquidated. The company's authorised capital was also reduced from £400,000 to £325,000 and its paid up capital from £275,000 to £200,000 by repaying 7,500 preference shares of £10 each.

During the General Strike of 1926, a record of over 1 million tons of coal was imported at Dagenham from all over Europe to supply London's power stations. The strike was called by the Trades Union Congress in support of the miners, who were being forced to accept lower wages for longer hours. Although the General Strike lasted only nine days in May 1926, the miners continued strike action until the end of the year when forced back to work by starvation. There is a story that when a group of London strikers arrived at Dagenham to stop the powerhouse working, they were turned back by the foreman Jim Coe who was well known for his boxing skills. He successfully defended the door and the powerhouse continued to work.

In 1927 William Varco Williams retired as Chairman due to ill health and was succeeded by his brother Arthur Edward Williams. In 1928 further financial adjustments saw Samuel Williams' authorised and paid up share capital reduced to £200,000 by repaying 12,500 preference shares of £10 each. Two years later its authorised capital was increased to £250,000, doubling in 1936 to £500,000.

1936 saw an agreement between Samuel Williams & Sons and the London Power Company, that Dagenham be used as an emergency stockpile for coal. During the summer months coal stocks would be built up so that during the winter, when colliers might be held up due to bad weather, the power stations could be fed from Dagenham. It was felt that the No. 4 jetty was inadequate for the task so a new jetty, No. 7, was built to the west of the "Thunderer" jetty. The decision to stockpile at Dagenham was farsighted, even then it was believed war would break out in Europe and London's supply of energy would have to be maintained at all costs. After the war the coal heaps were gradually replaced by oil tanks as oil superseded coal as a power source. The coal heaps never completely disappeared and in time became covered in vegetation. At about the same time the company acquired the coal business of H Harrison (Shipping) Ltd, which also operated a small coastal collier fleet which passed to the management of William Coe, Liverpool.

INTO SHIPOWNING (1915 to 1939)

John Hudson & Co Ltd ordered its first ship from the Campbeltown Shipbuilding Co Ltd. Campbeltown is on the west coast of Scotland near the southern tip of the Kintyre peninsula. Launched on 3 March 1915 as **Oxshott**, she was a shelter deck steamer of 761 net tons powered by a triple expansion steam engine built by Rankin & Blackmore Ltd, Greenock. Credited with a speed of nine knots she often made ten or eleven knots and was referred to as "the North East Flyer". Completed two months later she was the only ship built for the company by this yard, probably because the more traditional east coast collier builders were busy with Admiralty contracts. She was named after the Surrey village where Samuel Williams' son Alfred lived. Until the outbreak of World War 2, company policy was to name ships after places associated with the company or the Williams family.

The company expanded the fleet the following year with the building of another two colliers. Both ships came from the Sunderland yard of Osbourne, Graham & Co Ltd which had built many colliers. The first, in September 1916, was named **Hornchurch** (1) and was a steamship of 1301 net tons. The following year her sister was completed as **Upminster** (1) and entered service in March 1917. **Hornchurch** (1) became the company's only loss during World War 1, on 3 August 1917 when her propeller struck a mine laid by the German submarine **UC 29** three and a half miles from Coquet Island off the Northumberland coast. At the time she was in ballast from the Thames for Methil and sank with the loss of two of her crew. No further additions were made to the fleet until the end of the war.

In 1919 John Hudson & Co Ltd took the opportunity to purchase three ships ordered during the war by the Shipping Controller from Osbourne, Graham & Co which, because of the end of hostilities, were now surplus to Government requirements. Launched as **War Browny** and **War Ness**, the first two ships were bought while fitting out and completed in late 1919 as **Hornchurch** (2) and **Dagenham**. The third ship had been laid down as **War Boyne** but at the time of her sale to the company had not been launched and was subsequently launched as **Lolworth**. **Hornchurch** (2) and **Dagenham** were sisters of 1250 net tons while **Lolworth** was slightly smaller at 1150 net tons. At the time of her completion **Lolworth**'s dimensions were the maximum that could berth in Seaham, County Durham, where she often loaded coal. **Dagenham** and **Hornchurch** (2) loaded mainly from the Tyne at Northumberland Dock, at Methil, or occasionally at Leith. On entering service **Hornchurch**'s Master and Chief Engineer were Captain Howat and Mr W Hunter who had served on **Hornchurch** (1) at the time of her loss in 1917.

Lolworth was the last ship to be built for John Hudson & Co Ltd. While she was fitting out the Hudson Steamship Co Ltd was formed on 13 April 1920 to own and manage the fleet. At the same time the opportunity was taken to wind up John Hudson & Co Ltd. A new company with the same title was incorporated and traded solely as coal agents.

On its formation the Hudson Steamship Co Ltd board comprised five directors. The first Chairman was Samuel Williams' youngest son Arthur Edward Williams. The other directors were his brother Alfred Williams, Colonel Frank Ainslie Williams OBE, Alfred Williams' son, and Captain Herbert Edward Ingle who was the eldest child of Samuel Williams' daughter, Annie. The only non-family member of the board was John Robertson, a director of John Hudson & Co Ltd and Samuel Williams & Sons Ltd. The Company Secretary was Mr E M Rowntree. Within group circles the company was referred to either as 'Hudson Steamship' or 'Steamship'. Because of this, it is referred to as such in the this book.

When formed, Hudson Steamship shared its offices with John Hudson & Co Ltd at 25 Billiter Street. In 1925, both companies moved, along with Samuel Williams & Sons Ltd, to 8 Lloyds Avenue, London EC3, which became the headquarters of the three associated companies. The new company inherited a fleet of five relatively new steamers, and as trading conditions remained uncertain due to the depression no further additions were made to the fleet. However in 1928 **Upminster** (1) was lost. On 2 May she was in collision in dense fog with the steamer **Lanrick** fifteen miles south of Flamborough Head. Commanded by Captain R Proudley, she was in ballast from London for Methil. At 8pm she was run down by **Lanrick** which was bound for Ghent. **Lanrick** suffered a twisted stem and was able to take off the crew of **Upminster**, whose fore part was under water but still afloat, and landed them at Immingham. The tug **Lynx** was sent to the casualty which sank before any salvage attempt could be made. Even in view of her loss a replacement ship was not ordered for another six years, such were the trading conditions at the time.

In 1934 a contract was signed with the Burntisland Shipbuilding Co Ltd, Burntisland, for the construction of a 1400dwt steamship. She differed from the existing fleet as she was a raised quarterdeck vessel with engines aft whereas previous ships had been built with bridge and engines amidships. Delivered in late 1934 as **Upminster** (2), she entered the London house coal trade where she proved a successful ship. She was the first in the company to be fitted with a radio telegraphy set, and the first ship in the company to regularly load cargo from Blyth. Four years later the company returned to her builders with an order for a sister ship which was delivered in early 1938 as **Brasted**, for the same trade as her sister.

*A fascinating view of the **Upminster** (2) taken at an unidentified Thames wharf on 20 March 1938. The quayside industrial archaeology is of great interest.*

(Norton Crockett)

In 1934 Mr E M Rowntree was succeeded as Company Secretary by Mr William J Crafter, who became a director of the company in 1954. Mr Crafter also held the position of Secretary for both Samuel Williams & Sons Ltd and John Hudson & Co Ltd. He had joined Samuel Williams & Sons in 1924 as Chief Accountant. Also joining the board in 1934 were Arthur Lawrence Williams and Samuel Walter (Sam) Williams. Both were sons of Arthur Edward Williams. Three years later Alfred Williams left the board on 31 March 1937. He was succeeded the following month by Lionel Gardner Locket who, in time, was also Managing Director of John Hudson & Co Ltd and a director of Samuel Williams & Sons Ltd. On 30 September 1939, Arthur Williams retired as Chairman and was succeeded by his son Arthur Lawrence Williams.

The 1919-built **Hornchurch** outward bound in the Thames estuary on 13 May 1939.

(Norton Crockett)

Life on board a pre-war collier is described by Mr W J Crafter's son Edmund who made several trips on Hudson Steamship's colliers from the Thames to load coal in the north east. He eventually joined Samuel Williams & Sons in 1948 in the Accounting Department and retired in 1985 from the post of Operations Manager in John Hudson & Co Ltd.

"In 1935 during the summer vacation, my father arranged for myself and a friend to spend a trip from the Thames to Methil on **Hornchurch** (2) to load coal. We had to report to Lloyds Avenue where the manager of Hudson Steamship took us by taxi to the ship which was to sail from Deptford. During late afternoon and evening we sailed down the Thames Estuary in beautiful sunshine. Meals were with the Captain, 1st and 2nd Mates, the Engineers and Sparks, the Wireless Operator, who would use Morse to communicate with the shore stations. Our first meal would be around 6pm. I can remember asking for the sugar and no one took any notice, only to be told 'You don't ask, you stretch' - a new experience as I was always taught to say 'please and thank you'. Tea was very strong and canned milk was used, I didn't like it very much, but by the time I was in the army, 1939-1946, I soon found it acceptable.

Captain Howat was skipper of **Hornchurch** (2) and he had his wife on board for the trip. The first mate had a bald patch on the top of his head and I understood that the reason for this was because he was forever spitting into his cap. As he chewed tobacco and then replaced the cap on his head it probably caused his hair to rot. I was intrigued watching him make a hammock out of sail cloth which he strung up for Mrs Howat on the deck below the chart room where we two boys had our quarters. I slept on a chartroom table and my pal on the bench. We only had blankets, no luxuries such as a mattress. On our first day at sea I was seasick. The steward was to take care of our welfare, he would say that if there was anything good in your stomach the sea will have it out. When he felt I could manage nourishment, he brought a large mug of steaming soup, and by Jove did I enjoy it. On one occasion I couldn't make the side of the ship and all I had to offer went on the chart room bridge deck. However, the steward soon had a bucket of water to flush the offending sight down the scuppers. At the mess table later, I was given a strange look. It wasn't until later that I learnt that the bucket of water, etc, had met the wind and had been blown back onto the hammock below.

Life on board was full of interest. Mind you, everything was very basic. Some of the sailors were Lascars; their quarters were in the foc'sle; they slept in hammocks and their urinal was a bucket at the foot of the companionway.

At Methil we were met by a representative from Matthew Taylor and given a local tour and went into Edinburgh sightseeing. We returned to the ship the next day after loading and sailed back to the Thames. I was given 10 shillings to pay the steward for my week's vitals whilst on board and bought him 100 Players cigarettes as a thank you. They cost me 4s 11d. That trip remains with me as a wonderful experience.

Between 1936 and 1939, I sailed on **Upminster** (2), **Dagenham** and **Oxshott.** The skipper of **Upminster** (2) was Captain Brown who I remember never slept in his bunk while at sea, and I was lucky as I was invited to use his bunk. He sat and slept in an armchair in the mess room. Captain Proudly of the **Oxshott** had the ability to sail through bad weather and fog. At that time there was no radar, and the ship was nicknamed 'The Ghost Ship', it always seemed to get through. If the visibility was poor, no-one talked; they just listened.

Other than Methil and/or Leven in Scotland there was the "Howden Dock" on the Tyne. The manager of John Hudson & Co Ltd was very kind and I remember being shown Howden Dock, mainly built of timber where the coal trucks would rumble down the track and tip their contents onto a shute and into the ship's hold. As soon as the ship sailed, the wooden hatch covers would be replaced and when at sea hoses would be used to flush coal spilt on the deck overboard. I always felt that this was a waste but it was cheaper to do this than use labour to shovel it into a hold. Coal was extremely cheap in the 1930s."

WORLD WAR 2

At the outbreak of war the company operated a fleet of six ships with an average age of just over eleven years, yet four of these had traded for the company for more than twenty years each. By the end of the war only two of the fleet survived. Supplying London and the south-east of England with coal was a hazardous task made worse with the fall of France. The collier fleets faced the threat of mines, E-boats and air attacks while those ships sailing through the Dover Straits to the south coast ports were subjected to attack from German shore based artillery in occupied France.

The convoy system was very quickly adopted. The first southbound convoy sailed from Methil on 6 September 1939. Convoys were designated FS for southbound and FN for northbound. All southbound convoys originated from Methil with ships joining from ports such as Amble, Blyth, Tyne, Seaham, etc down to the Humber as the convoy passed. Independent sailings were attempted but were soon abandoned due to high losses. There were two types of convoys, fast where the ships were capable of ten knots and slow with ships capable of eight knots or less. Most of the east coast colliers sailed in the slow convoys. It was quite often the case that a convoy was strung out over a fair number of miles due to the Commodore ship being a fast ship and under orders to be at a prearranged place at a set time. Joining ships would take position behind the last ship in either port or starboard column depending on their orders. Off the Norfolk coast E-boats would tie up alongside the route buoys waiting for a convoy, not detectable to the few escorts fitted with radar. The favourite tactic was to attack between the two columns, making it difficult for ships to fire in case they hit a ship in the opposite column.

An example of the early convoys was FN 11 in which **Hornchurch** (2), under the command of Captain Howat, acted as Commodore ship. The convoy of twenty four ships assembled off Southend at 1030 on 26 September 1939. The convoy was to proceed in single file until it met with its three escorting vessels, the warships **Bittern**, **Enchantress** and **Broke**, in the Barrow Deep when it would form into two columns of twelve. The columns were to be three cables apart with the distance between each ship in the column two cables. Should the convoy come under air attack the orders were to turn outward ninety degrees and reform as soon as the attack was over. Vessels leaving the convoy were to do so at the outer ends of swept channels for those ports.

Hornchurch (2) was lead ship in the starboard column with the Vice Commodore's vessel **Joseph Swan** (1571grt/38) commanded by Captain Reid opposite in the port column. Vessels in the convoy represented many of the collier owners at the time including France Fenwick, Cory, and the Newcastle companies Newbiggin SS Co and Witherington & Everett.

After a day steaming the first vessel to leave the convoy did so at the Humber Light Vessel. Another, **Hamsterley**, joined for passage to the Firth of Forth. As the convoy headed further north so ships dropped out, the convoy being arranged that ships dropped back from the columns as they passed their destinations. Eight ships were for the Tyne and five for Blyth; they left in the early hours of 28 September, leaving **Hornchurch** (2) and two others for the Firth of Forth. **Hornchurch** (2) arrived at Methil at 1330 on 28 September and in his report Captain Howat stated the station keeping of the convoy was good although several vessels had difficulty maintaining the required eight knots.

The first few months of the war saw no loss for the company, although 1940 proved to be a disastrous year for ships and men lost. In the first seven months of that year three were sunk. The first came on 10 January when **Upminster** (2) was lost off Haisborough Sand on passage from Methil for London with 1350 tons of coal. Having sailed from Methil on 4 January she arrived in the Tyne the following day to pick up a southbound convoy. However she sailed on the morning of Monday 8 January alone. There was a delay in sailing as the crew had stated they wished to sail in a convoy which did not materialise.

At 1000 on 9 January she was attacked by two German aircraft, believed to be Heinkel 111s, two to three miles south-east of the Hammond Knoll Light Vessel. The aircraft approached from ahead of the ship, one on each side, and machine gunned the bridge, crossfiring into the wheelhouse. They circled and one dropped a bomb on the focsle head, blowing it right off and killing a crew member inside. The forward bulkhead remained intact and kept the ship afloat while she zig-zagged to avoid the planes. Another bomb exploded on the bridge killing Captain A Hunter and the lookout. The aircraft continued to machine gun the vessel as her crew abandoned. They counted six bombs dropped on **Upminster** (2). Three missed, the third hitting the fore deck starboard side. The crew members lost were J Stubbs and W R Young. The survivors were rescued from the boat after half an hour by the steamer **Ngarmo** and landed at Great Yarmouth.

In the early morning of 10 January, the Cromer lifeboat **H F Bailey** commanded by Coxswain Henry Blogg was launched to assist an unidentified steamer reported bombed north-east of Cromer. They located **Upminster** (2) in a sinking condition. Some of the lifeboat crew boarded her and found her abandoned with women's shoes scattered about her deck. The lifeboat stood by as a salvage tug had been sent from the Humber. She later sank in position 53.03N 01.29E. The lifeboat then searched the area and found one of **Upminster**'s empty lifeboats and towed it back to Cromer.

Two months later on 23 April **Lolworth** struck a mine near Elbow Buoy and sank. In ballast from Portsmouth for the Tyne, she was serving as a naval collier, having been requisitioned some months earlier. Of her crew of twenty one, plus two naval gunners, Mr R Wickman, her 2nd Mate, and Chief Engineer J O Hunter were lost and a further eight injured.

Her master Captain A Tomlinson, in an interview about the loss, reported that at 1750 BST the vessel was about half a mile west of Elbow Light Buoy off Broadstairs, Kent, in about five fathoms of water holding a steady course at a speed of nine knots. The weather was clear, sea smooth with a light northerly wind, when he heard a dull thud. At the time he was on the starboard side of the upper bridge. The ship sustained damage under her bridge to port with the side being blown away. Captain Tomlinson was knocked out by debris and regained consciousness as water poured down on him. The ship's funnel was down and her steward who was by the cabin on the starboard side before the explosion found himself in the bunkers. The Second Mate who had walked to the port side of the bridge prior to the explosion was never seen again. The starboard side of the ship was bent out and the ship was listing to port and the crew could not lower the starboard lifeboat. The mate reported that the port side lifeboat was in the water and Captain Tomlinson only abandoned his ship when her deck was level with the lifeboat in which were himself and sixteen crew. Two other crew and the two naval gunners were later picked up from a raft by a trawler and transferred to a naval motor launch which landed them at Ramsgate.

Hornchurch (2) was the next ship lost. She sailed from Methil under the command of Captain Howat with 2930 tons of coal on 10 July 1940 as Commodore ship in her convoy. After picking up ships from the Tyne the convoy proceeded south, the weather deteriorating with heavy rain and poor visibility. By now a Naval Commodore had taken charge and *Hornchurch* (2) took position as third ship in the starboard column. Regarded as the first major east coast convoy battle of the war, enemy aircraft were sighted at 0833 and were fired upon by the escorts. At 0845 with the convoy about six miles off the coast nine German aircraft attacked. A salvo of bombs were aimed at the leading destroyer, *Wallace*, and the formation then attacked the convoy from starboard, straddling *Hornchurch* with a string of bombs. Fifty five minutes later the convoy was attacked again and *Hornchurch* was struck by a salvo of bombs in a position 52.11 15N, 01.52 30E. Her crew of twenty-two abandoned ship, rescued by the warship *Widgeon*. *Hornchurch* later sank near the Aldeburgh Light vessel having drifted approximately two miles inshore to a position 52.11 30N 51.45E. Fortunately there was no loss of life among her crew. Her radio officer, who had served aboard for nearly fourteen years later went on to be senior radio officer aboard *Dominion Monarch*.

On 16 November 1940, *Dagenham*, commanded by Captain D W Brown, struck a mine approximately 2.5 cables ENE of the Mouse Light Vessel, inward from Methil for the Thames. Sailing in Convoy FS 335, she was Commodore for the single file convoy and at the time of the incident was lead ship, armed with a 12-pounder and a Lewis gun. At about 1340 she passed over a magnetic mine which exploded. Prior to the explosion two trawlers had passed about three miles ahead on exactly the same course. *Dagenham* proceeded for another fifteen minutes until she met the examination vessel, all the time settling deeper in the water with her lifeboats blown out of their davits and hanging over the side. It was then that Captain Brown decided that he should try and ground his vessel to stop her from sinking.

Dagenham was beached in about four fathoms on the Barrow Sands in a position 220 degrees and 11 cables from the East Cant Buoy in the Thames estuary. Captain Brown sent the crew ashore as there was no accommodation for them although he retained the officers and engineers. They stayed in the chart and wireless room once they had made sure it would not flood. The following morning all, except Captain Brown, were taken off.

As she had been beached in an unfavourable position attempts were made to move her although her keel was pinned aft after being beached, and her engine and boiler rooms were flooded. Operations on 18 November only resulted in her being towed a further two cables. A later attempt to pump out the engine and boiler rooms failed. It was estimated 600 tons of coal would have to be discharged from No 4 hold to help salve her. At this time her after deck, aft end of the fore deck and halfway up her coaming were flooded at high water.

*A fine view of the **Dagenham** underway in ballast, probably outward bound in the Thames estuary.*

(W H Brown, World Ship Photo Library)

At 1630 on 21 November she was refloated, although still leaking and was beached on Grain Island during the night of 21/22 November. Salvage pumps gradually gained control as leaks in her hull were plugged by divers. During the night of 23/24, an attempt to refloat her failed, due to an insufficient rise in the tide, and two days later it was reported her stern was afloat but she was aground forward. On the morning of the 27th, she was refloated and passed Gravesend at 1025 in tow of a tug, attended by the salvage steamers *Gauntlet* and *Daunt*. Discharge of cargo began later that day at Rainham.

There were no casualties amongst her crew of twenty-two, one DEMS gunner, Commodore and three RN ratings. The company lost her services for nearly six months while she was repaired. During the war she often sailed as Commodore ship and was always at the van of the convoy due to her speed, eleven knots.

The company was appointed managers of two ageing steamers in October 1940. As a result of Russia annexing the Baltic States in 1940, the Ministry of War Transport took over these countries' ships. Both the Latvian **Elizabete** and the Estonian **Vilk**, were employed on the east coast. **Elizabete** was a 1917 American-built steamer while **Vilk** came from Sunderland in 1913 for William Cory.

The following year the company was able to purchase from Welsh owners two second-hand steamers built in the early 1920s. Due to wartime restrictions they were not renamed. **Bramhill**, was built in 1923 for Newport owner Mordey, Son & Co Ltd as **Gwentland**. In 1936 she was sold to Claude Angel, Mordey replacing her with a smaller newbuilding, and renamed **Bramhill**. For the next two years she regularly traded to Spain, supplying Republican forces fighting General Franco in the Civil War. Her record deserves mention. On 12 January 1937 she was fired on by the trawler **Larache** while on passage from Barcelona to Bilbao via Tarragona with general cargo. Her master wirelessed for help and the call was answered by the cruiser **HMS Sussex**, which, on arrival, requested the trawler to leave. **Bramhill**'s papers were inspected by the captain of the **Sussex**, and the ship was eventually allowed to continue.

*A very early photograph of the **Bramhill** arriving to load at a port in the north-east of England. The loading staithes are barely visible in the background.*

(George Scott)

This was not the first nor the only incident involving **Bramhill**. In October 1936 Franco's forces claimed she had been unloading ammunition at Alicante. On 16 August 1937 she sailed from Gijon for France with refugees from the conflict. At the same time the steamer **Nailsea Vale** sailed from Aviles, the two ships evacuating 5,600 people. Upon her return to Spain she was intercepted on 28 August by two insurgent trawlers off Gijon. When fired upon her master did not stop as he considered himself in international waters. The ship was fired upon again whereupon **HMS Fearless** arrived on the scene and confirmed **Bramhill** was in international waters. **Bramhill** continued to seaward and the incident was closed. **Bramhill** was damaged on two occasions during the Civil War, the first at Buriana in December 1937 when she was damaged during shelling of the port by Nationalist ships. On 22 July 1938 while discharging at Gandia in company with another of Angel's fleet, **Dellwyn**, a cache of fifty bombs exploded 200 yards away from the quay. **Bramhill** was undamaged and sailed shortly after. While lying at Barcelona on 8 October 1938 with a cargo of beans and beer **Bramhill** was hit by a bomb from a Nationalist seaplane which attacked the port late in the evening. This caused an eight foot hole in the deck amidships. She also sustained damage above the waterline from bombs exploding on the quayside and in the water.

Also purchased from Newport owners was **Macbrae** of Guardian Line Ltd. Built at Burntisland for Grahamstown Shipping Co Ltd, Glasgow, she was sold to Guardian Line in 1937. Although renamed, her new owners did not change her port of registry which was not unusual for Welsh owners as it saved money on fees. **Macbrae** was the last ship owned by Guardian, the company ceasing trading shortly after her sale.

Such was the value of ships at the time that Hudson Steamship paid £40,000 for **Bramhill**, which had been sold for £10,250 in 1936. **Macbrae** was purchased for £52,500 when five years previously she had been sold for £32,500. Although the sale of **Macbrae** was arranged in September 1941 the vessel was on His Majesty's Service mainly trading on the west coast of Scotland and was not handed over until December 1941. She remained requisitioned until 9 November 1942.

The company suffered only the loss of **Oxshott** in 1941. Having loaded a cargo of coal at Seaham for Dagenham she was in Convoy FS 69 escorted by the warships **Vimera** and **Wolsey**, supported by armed trawlers. Because of the threat of mines in the narrow channels the convoy routes were constantly switched off the Norfolk coast. The route buoys in that area were switched on by radio signals when the convoy approached and off when the last ship had passed. On the night of 6/7 August, as a result of poor visibility due to a north north-westerly gale and with squalls of wind and rain, **Oxshott** and six other vessels in the convoy found themselves hard aground on Haisborough Sand off the Norfolk coast in position 52.54 30N, 01.43 50E. It was believed that in the poor visibility the vessels did not read the Aldis message to alter course. By 0930 on the morning of the 7th when RNLI lifeboats reached the ships only the masts, funnel and upper works of **Oxshott** were visible.

The Cromer lifeboat **H F Bailey**, with Coxswain Henry Blogg, thought the crew had abandoned **Oxshott** before they had arrived and turned towards another wreck. Fortunately one of the lifeboat crew noticed sixteen of her crew on the upperworks. The ship was breaking up and there was no way the lifeboat could get a line aboard. Blogg decided to place the lifeboat's bows in a wedge shaped opening in the ship's superstructure. Although the seas pushed the lifeboat away several times the lifeboat regained position. Sixteen survivors were taken off **Oxshott**, and thirty one from the French steamer **Gallois** (2684grt/17). Eventually the men were transferred to a destroyer and **H F Bailey** continued the rescue in company with the second Cromer boat, **Harriet Dixon**, and lifeboats from Sheringham, Gorleston and Lowestoft. Captain Howat who had been in command of both **Hornchurch** (1) and **Hornchurch** (2), when they were lost, and four crew members died as a result.

About a dozen ships had grounded before the following collier skippers realised the navigation error and steered clear. A total of eight ships were lost in the incident. *Oxshott* and *Gallois* as mentioned, France Fenwick's steamer *Deerwood* (1914grt/19), *Aberhill* (1516grt/15), *Afon Towey* (684grt/19), Stephenson Clarke's *Betty Hindley* (1738grt/41) on her maiden voyage and the Estonian *Taara* (1402grt/07). The anti-submarine trawler *HMS Agate*, formerly the Fleetwood trawler *Mavis Rose* (627grt/34), was also lost. During his thirty nine years as coxswain of the Cromer lifeboat Henry Blogg helped save 873 lives, winning an unequalled three RNLI gold and four silver medals. Two ships were added to the fleet during 1942. *Philipp M*, a 1924-built sister to *Macbrae*, was purchased from the Mooringwell Steamship Co Ltd for £54,000 in September and handed over in December. The Mooringwell Steamship Co had been formed in 1936, one of its directors being a pitwood importer. The company was an extension of his business. Coal was shipped from South Wales to France and pitwood imported on the return voyage.

Both *Philipp M* and *Macbrae* were "archdeck" steamers built to the Ayre-Ballard patent. The principle of this design meant the hull strength came from incorporating a longitudinal inverse sheer with a transverse arch. The inverse sheer, a scientific engineering design found in many bridges, resulted in the deck amidships being about 7 feet higher than usual, hence no midship structure was required. The other obvious feature was the inward curve of the upper sides of the ship. The design used 10-14% less steel and the holds were free of pillars and beams, ideal for bulk cargo such as timber and coal. Despite their advantages only 28 ships were built to the design between 1911 and 1928. Hudson were also awarded management of a collier on behalf of the Ministry of War Transport. *Empire Lagoon* belonged to a class of twenty six ships of about 2,800 dwt known as the "Icemaid" class as they were based on the collier *Icemaid* completed in 1936 for the Gas, Light & Coke Co, London.

No ships were lost in 1942 and 1943 and it was not until February 1944 that the company lost another, *Philipp M* off Great Yarmouth. Under the command of Captain M Hunter she sailed from the Tyne on 23 February with 3102 tons of coal for the Thames, as Vice Commodore in Convoy FS 1371. She was armed with four Oerlikons, a Lewis gun, 2 PAC rockets and also flew a balloon. One RN signaller and four DEMS gunners were carried in addition to her crew of twenty. At 2334 on the 24th, the escorting destroyer sent a message advising there were E-boats in the area. A minute later, when approximately two miles north of the Hearty Knoll Buoy, a torpedo struck the vessel. She was steering a course 5½° E at a speed of three knots.

Previous to the ship being hit, the Second Officer reported an E-boat to starboard which approached at high speed from aft on a parallel course before stopping her engines and lying next to a sand bank to the north of Hearty Knoll. At the time the Second Officer could not distinguish if this was an E-boat or a RN torpedo boat. He later concluded it must have been this E-boat which fired the torpedo. The ship was struck on the starboard side amidships and the engine room began to flood immediately. The flash from the explosion was seen by a northbound convoy three miles away. There were no lifeboats left intact so the crew abandoned using two rafts. The crew on the starboard raft were later rescued by *Lady Olga* which dropped her jollyboat to pick up those in the water and then the raft. *Lady Olga* had earlier come across the crew from the port raft but had been unable to stop in time although one gunlayer managed to jump from the raft onto the scrambling nets. However there was a motor launch behind which picked up the crew and landed them at Southend.

Captain Hunter, the Chief and Third Engineers, a Donkeyman and the bo'sun were lost along with one of the Army gunners when she sank in 52.45N, 2.12E, while the steward died aboard *Lady Olga*. Three other crew were injured. Captain Hunter had survived the sinking of three ships previous to *Philipp M*. The E-boats which attacked the convoy were believed to belong to the 2nd and 8th Flotillas engaged on a minelaying operation. To replace her the company purchased *Hetton* from the Tanfield Steamship Co Ltd, Newcastle, built by S P Austin & Sons Ltd, Sunderland in 1924. The company also took over management of a sister to *Empire Lagoon*. Previously managed by Wm Cory, *Empire Pioneer* had been built by the Ailsa Shipbuilding Co Ltd, Troon. During 1944 the company lost the services of three owned ships when *Dagenham*, *Bramhill* and *Hetton* were requisitioned for service during the Normandy Landings. *Empire Lagoon* and the former Estonian *Vilk* were the first ships operated by the company to arrive at the Normandy beachheads. *Empire Lagoon* sailed in Convoy ETC2Z from London for the Eastern Task Force Area while *Vilk* sailed from London in Convoy ETC2Y for the same location, both ships arriving there on 7 June.

Dagenham and *Hetton* made their first trip to Normandy in convoy ETC 8 a week after D-Day, loading ammunition at Tilbury for Sword and Gold beaches respectively. Prior to the invasion *Dagenham* had been operating in the Humber and Dover areas. Requisitioned on 3 May, *Bramhill* sailed in Convoy EBC 10 on 12 June from Swansea and arrived at Omaha beach on 16 June. Later in June, *Dagenham* returned to unload cargo at Caen and Arromanches. All three owned ships were returned to the company by the end of the year, although *Bramhill* suffered severe bottom damage when run aground on the beachhead. It had been found that by beaching coasters they could be discharged more effectively at low water. It was during these operations that *Dagenham*'s master, Captain Brown, collapsed from exhaustion. He was brought home by the naval authorities but later died, and was subsequently awarded a posthumous British Empire Medal. He had been master of *Dagenham* when she had been mined near Barrow Sands in 1940 and against advice had insisted on taking his ship to Normandy. *Empire Pioneer* also made several trips to Normandy in November 1944 and the following summer discharged cargo in Antwerp, Rotterdam and northern France.

At the end of hostilities, only *Brasted* and *Dagenham* survived from the six ships owned by Hudson Steamship in September 1939. Like other companies, Hudson now began a programme of reconstruction. Management of the two Estonian ships on behalf of the Ministry of Transport was retained until the 1950s. Another Estonian vessel, *Miervaldis*, was also managed for a short time in 1948 and in September that year was one of seventeen obsolete ships scuttled in the Bay of Biscay in an operation to dispose of chemical weapons.

POST WAR RECONSTRUCTION

At the end of the war Hudson Steamship controlled a fleet of nine ships, five being owned and four managed on behalf of the Ministry of War Transport which later became the Ministry of Transport. Of the five owned ships, four were over twenty years old with only the **Brasted** being less than ten years old. Like other collier owners, Hudson Steamship had suffered on the exposed east coast supplying London and the south coast ports. The company now implemented a modernisation plan by placing orders for two colliers with the Ailsa Shipbuilding Co Ltd, Troon.

Under the Government's Ship Disposal Scheme which allowed owners to buy ships owned by the Ministry of War Transport, the company purchased the **Empire Lagoon** and **Empire Pioneer** which were respectively renamed **Hudson Bay** in November 1945 and **Hudson Bank** in February 1946. To help fund this reconstruction and other business activities, Samuel Williams' authorised capital was increased to £950,000 in July 1947.

Hudson Bay outward bound from the River Tyne with the huge premises of British Ropes Limited dominating the far side of the river.

(World Ship Photo Library)

Three of the pre-war steamers were sold to new owners during 1946. The **Brasted** was sold to Guernsey shipowner Onesimus Dorey early in the year. The **Bramhill** was sold to the Shamrock Shipping Co Ltd, Larne, and arrived in Belfast on 25 April after loading a positioning cargo of coal at Blyth, sailing via Dunnet on the Pentland Firth. In October, the **Hetton** was sold to Chinese owners and traded for another twelve years before she was broken up.

One incident worthy of mention at this time concerned the Ministry of War Transport managed **Elizabete** which was involved in a salvage operation in the North Atlantic. On 1 August 1946, the American vessel **American Farmer** loaded with general cargo for London from Baltimore was in collision with another American ship, **William J Riddle**, some seven hundred miles west of the Lizard. **American Farmer** was struck in the area of No 2 hatch and, down by the head but still afloat, was abandoned by her crew. Soon after **American Farmer** was abandoned, a sistership, **American Traveller**, arrived intending to tow her to port. Unable to take the tow, she left the casualty. Two days later another sistership, **American Ranger**, reported that having boarded the drifting derelict and, before a towing connection could be made, **Elizabete** had arrived, made tow ropes secure and had proceeded to tow **American Farmer**.

More of **American Ranger**'s crew boarded the casualty, severed the tow with **Elizabete** and forced the British crew to leave. One report claimed the American destroyer **Perry** advised **Elizabete** that she should leave the scene. **American Farmer**'s engines were restarted and she arrived in Falmouth Bay on 8 August. The incident caused uproar and resulted in a court case with claims and counter claims between the parties concerned. **American Farmer** returned to service and was eventually broken up in May 1969.

The first newbuilding ordered from the Troon yard was launched on 27 June 1946 by Mrs E J K Goldsmith, wife of one of the company's directors as **Hudson Strait**. She was the first of twenty-eight colliers of around 4500dwt delivered between 1945 and 1956, the majority being for the British Electricity Authority (BEA) which was created in April 1948. The **Hudson Strait** and her subsequent sisterships **Hudson River** and **Hudson Firth**, differed from other new colliers in having five holds while the others had only four. Hudson Steamship's vessels spent most of their careers on charter to John Hudson & Co Ltd whilst other owners arranged long-term charters with the BEA. The Hudson ships often carried different grades of coal and five holds gave them greater flexibility. In December 1946, for example, 800 tons of opencast coal was loaded at Blyth by the **Hudson Strait**, this being the first consignment of opencast coal from the port. The **Hudson Strait** ran trials in October 1946 achieving a speed of 11.29 knots. On 24 October 1946, the **Hudson Cape** was launched at Troon by Mrs A E Minns. At 293 ft, this vessel was 32 ft shorter than **Hudson Strait** and had only four holds. She had a deadweight of 3561 tonnes. After completing trials, she was handed over to the company in December 1946.

*Hudson River (above) and **Hudson Firth** (below). As described on page 14, the **Hudson Firth** differed in several ways from her near-sister. Most obvious in this photograph is the provision of cargo handling gear on the **Hudson Firth**, and there are several other differences evident at the stern of the vessel.*

(Both photographs by Skyfotos and in author's collection)

During 1948, orders for a further three ships were placed with the Ailsa yard. Two were similar to the **Hudson Strait** and one was a sister of the **Hudson Cape**. The **Hudson River** was launched in April 1949 and was handed over in August that year; she was followed by the **Hudson Firth** which entered service in December 1949. **Hudson River** was identical to **Hudson Strait** and was completed as a coal-burning gearless steam collier. During the construction of **Hudson Firth**, the company had decided to diversify away from the collier trade and the decision was taken to fit her with oil fired boilers and increased bunker capacity allowing her to trade further afield. She was also fitted with cargo handling derricks.

The formation of the BEA resulted in the creation of a nationalised collier fleet and the company felt that charters for its own colliers might not be renewed. Hudson Steamship therefore arranged a charter with Tate & Lyle Ltd for the carriage of bulk sugar from the West Indies. The **Hudson Firth** carried more sugar cargoes than coal during her career with Hudson Steamship. When she did carry coal, which was usually in winter, her derricks were stowed against her masts to assist loading at staithes. The **Hudson Firth**'s first cargoes were West Indies sugar to the United Kingdom and in 1950 she was sent to the Mediterranean, returning to Leith with esparto grass. Between 1953 and 1955, she worked in the north-east coast coal trade, loading predominantly at Hartlepool. She occasionally loaded export cargoes for Europe, and reverted to the sugar trade in 1956.

For most of their company service, the two ex-Empire ships and **Hudson River**, **Hudson Cape** and **Hudson Strait** were employed on charter to John Hudson & Co Ltd, carrying domestic and industrial types of coal loaded in the north east and Scottish ports. Discharge was either at Dagenham, Corys Wharf on Galleon Reach or at the Plastiboard berth at Erith. Only occasionally were they chartered to the British Electricity Authority, which in 1954 became the Central Electricity Authority. In 1958 the CEA became the Central Electricity Generating Board. With the arrival of new tonnage the company disposed of the ageing **Macbrae** to Middlesbrough owners in May 1949. She served her new owners for seven years before being sold again and was eventually lost in the Mediterranean in 1958.

The final ship to be delivered by Ailsa was launched as **Hudson Sound** in September 1950 and was handed over in December 1950. She was the same size as **Hudson Cape** and the company had decided to equip her with derricks and trade her in a similar way to the larger **Hudson Firth**. She was an oil-fired steamship with a daily consumption of 16.5 tons a day and a bunker capacity of 283 tons. She had a service speed of 10.5 knots. She was fitted with Mepco hatch covers on No 3 hatch. These were like roller shutters which stacked on the side deck whereas Macgregor covers would have been stowed at either end of the hatch. This enabled No 3 hatch to be larger than it would have been if fitted with Macgregor covers which were fitted to the other three hatches.

The cargo handling gear is evident in this view of the **Hudson Sound** *off the south coast of England. Unlike the* **Hudson Firth** *on the previous page, the* **Hudson Sound** *had only four hatches.*

(Skyfotos, author's collection)

Hudson Sound (1) was the final steamship built for the company and was designed for the Baltic and Mediterranean trades although like *Hudson Firth* she traded on the north-east coast during winter. All five Ailsa-built ships differed in appearance from other colliers built at this time as their stern accommodation was only at deck level, the other colliers having a two-block accommodation at the stern.

With the entry into service of *Hudson Sound* (1) the company owned a modern fleet of steamers with only *Dagenham* remaining from the pre-war fleet. The company ceased to be managers for *Vilk* in December 1950 when she was purchased by Cia Maritima La Villa S.A. who renamed her *La Villa* under the Panamanian flag. Since the end of the war she had operated on the east coast coal trade in winter, switching to the Baltic in summer although in September 1949 she had traded around Portugal and Spain.

*This wartime photograph of the **Vilk** should be compared to that of her in peacetime on page 82. Evident in the view here is the buoyant apparatus secured outboard of the mast.*

(A Duncan, WSPL)

In 1949, three of Hudson Steamship's directors became Joint Managing Directors of Samuel Williams & Sons in a move which saw the associated companies activities broken into manageable sizes. Mr J W Carmichael became responsible for the activities at Dagenham Dock with Mr K Goldsmith having responsibility for shipping. He was supported by Mr Walter Dallimore who was Shipping Manager based at Head Office. Mr A E Minns became responsible for industrial estate management, including commercial and industrial developments, which eventually led to the Williams' involvement in Vancouver Wharves in Canada. Together with the Managing Director of John Hudson & Co Ltd, Lionel Locket, who was associated with Charrington Gardner & Locket, these gentlemen were responsible for the development of Samuel Williams and associated companies until 1959 under the Chairmanship of Lawrence Williams.

*The **Hudson Sound** underway at full speed.*

(W Ralston)

1950s AND DIVERSIFICATION

At the beginning of the 1950s the company was in a very sound condition, owning a modern fleet of ships engaged in trade. After the experience gained operating **Hudson Firth** in the sugar trade the company decided to consider the possibility of constructing a larger bulk carrier for the same trade. In 1950 Tate & Lyle Ltd purchased **Empire Caicos**, a War Standard vessel of similar size to **Hudson Firth**, to carry West Indies sugar. Belonging to the **Empire Malta** class, she was a four hatch vessel designed with large hatchways and fitted with portable transverse sections at either end of the third hold. When removed this gave clear access to Number 2 and 4 holds allowing the ships to carry large vehicles or locomotives which due to their size could be loaded through one hatch. With her wide hatches and holds she was well suited to the carriage of sugar which was discharged by grabs. In 1951 Tate & Lyle purchased a sistership, **Thackeray** ex **Empire Aldgate**, and set about a building programme of owned vessels to run alongside chartered vessels.

After consultations between Hudson Steamship and Lloyd's Register of Shipping, and with technical advice from the company's marine superintendents, J W Dale & Sons Ltd, an order for a geared bulk carrier was placed with John Readhead & Sons Ltd, South Shields. An enlarged version of **Hudson Sound**, the new ship had a length of 434 feet and a deadweight of 8,000 tons. It was found possible to enlarge the earlier design of **Hudson Sound** by fitting constitute girders from aft under the bridge housing and forward to the forecastle, thus increasing the longitudinal strength. During her design, problems concerning trim under various conditions of loading, and the positioning of the bunkers had to be overcome.

At the time of her launch she was the world's largest raised threequarter deck type vessel afloat. She was the company's first motorship, being powered by a Doxford four-cylinder oil engine which gave a service speed of 12 knots on a consumption of 12 tons a day and she had a fuel oil bunker capacity of 744 tons. A five hatch vessel she differed in layout from **Hudson Firth** in having two hatches in the well deck and three hatches on the raised quarter deck. All hatches were fitted with steel covers. The holds had hopper sides to the tank tops to enable the hold corners to be cleared during discharge. Crew accommodation was to a high standard with an owner's cabin provided in the amidships housing. The stern accommodation included provision for four apprentices, the company looking to the training of future deck and engineering officers. As completed she was fitted with ten cargo derricks.

Launched by the wife of the company's chairman, Mrs A L Williams, on 23 April 1952 as **Hudson Deep** (1), she ran trials off the Northumberland coast on 29 August after loading a cargo of coal for the Thames in the Tyne. At the end of her trials the managing director of John Readhead & Sons Ltd, Mr G H R Towers, commented on the presence on board of a scientific team from the British Shipbuilding Research Association as observers during the trials and he hoped the results would add valuable knowledge to the design of future ships. E J K Goldsmith, managing director of Hudson Steamship, said the ship had been fixed on a three year charter with Tate & Lyle to carry sugar, but had also been designed to carry other bulk cargoes. A timber loadline had been assigned to the ship with special fitments having been incorporated in her building for the carrying of timber.

*A rather work-stained **Hudson Deep** moored to a buoy.*

(F Sherlock, WSPL)

Hudson Deep (1) discharged her cargo at Dagenham before ballasting to Cuba where she loaded her first sugar cargo. Her first master was Captain James Gibbons, DSC who had joined the company as relieving master in 1935. During World War 2 he served in the Royal Navy on the armed merchant cruiser *California* and later in minesweepers where he commanded *Bootle*. At the end of the war he returned to the company to command *Hetton*, *Vilk*, *Dagenham*, *Hudson Strait* and *Hudson Firth*. Whilst on one passage from the Tyne to the Thames, *Dagenham* was in collision with another ship and was holed. However she was safely berthed in the Thames and her cargo salved for which the underwriters publicly commended Captain Gibbons and other deck and engineer officers. Born in Whitehaven, Captain Gibbons obtained his First Mate's certificate in 1926 and his Master's certificate in 1931.

With the entry into service of *Hudson Deep* (1), the company had taken its first step to becoming a deepsea company, *Hudson Deep* being its first ship not intended for collier work. In October 1956 the company sold the ageing *Dagenham* after nearly thirty-seven years of service to Panamanian owners. During her time under company ownership, it was reckoned she made 1,352 voyages in the coal trade. A year later she was lost in the Black Sea. During 1952, the last ship managed on behalf of the Ministry of Transport, *Elizabete*, was sold to the Brila Shipping Co Ltd with Hudson Steamship remaining as her managers until 1956 when she was resold. She was eventually broken up after forty two years service in 1959. Like *Vilk*, she had operated in the east coast coal trade during winter and the Baltic in summer since the war. For the last eighteen months of her management, *Elizabete* had operated in the Baltic from July to December 1951 before switching to Portugal and Spain at the beginning of 1952, returning to the Baltic for the last half of the year.

In 1956, Samuel Williams & Sons Ltd became the Williams Hudson Group Ltd, a public company with an authorised capital of £1,450,000. At the same time a new holding company, John Hudson Fuel & Shipping Ltd, was created for both Hudson Steamship and John Hudson & Co Ltd. The new company was registered on 10 March 1956 with an initial share issue of one hundred £1 shares. In its original Articles of Association, the new company's business interests included colliery proprietors, iron masters and smelters, patent fuel manufacturers, shipowners, ship managers, barge owners and lightermen.

At an Extraordinary General Meeting on 29 March 1956, John Hudson Fuel & Shipping Ltd's shareholders passed three resolutions to increase the company's capital. The first saw the capital increased to £350,000 by the creation of 100,000 6% Cumulative Preference shares of £1 and 249,000 Ordinary £1 shares. This funded the purchase of John Hudson & Co Ltd. The second created a further 600,000 Ordinary £1 shares, increasing the capital to £950,000 for the purchase of Hudson Steamship shares. The third saw John Hudson Fuel & Shipping Ltd's capital rise to £1.2m by the issue of 250,000 unclassified £1 shares. The shareholdings purchased were £100,000 of 6% Preference and £200,000 Ordinary Stock in John Hudson & Co Ltd. and £308,000 ordinary stock in Hudson Steamship. In October 1956 a loan was taken out with the Pearl Assurance Co Ltd for £650,000 on a trust deed of 1% which was paid back by 1963. John Hudson Fuel & Shipping Ltd was incorporated on 10 July 1956 and the Williams family and other shareholders traded in their Hudson Steamship and John Hudson shares for shares in Fuel & Shipping. Both Hudson Steamship and Fuel & Shipping shared the same offices at 8 Lloyds Avenue, London EC3. The previous year Mr Lindsay Simpson had joined the board of Hudson Steamship. Four years later he was appointed Chairman of the company and also became Chairman of the Williams Hudson Group. In 1956 Mr L G Locket left the board of Hudson Steamship. Group profits saw a marked increase in the first year of trading. The various companies made a profit of £186,393 before tax in 1955 while in 1956, following restructuring and share issues, the group made £267,155 before tax. The value of the ships owned by Hudson Steamship was estimated at £897,328. One of the first actions of the company after this restructuring was to order a newbuilding in March 1956.

Contrasting with the previous photograph, the **Hudson Point** *is in excellent external condition in this fine photograph. She was either recently delivered or had just been drydocked.*

(Company achives)

The new ship was similar to **Hudson Deep** (1) but with larger capacity. The company again placed the order with John Readhead & Sons Ltd who, since the completion of **Hudson Deep**, had built similar sized ships for Stag Line and William France Fenwick. Named **Hudson Point**, she was launched by Mrs Fraser Parkes, granddaughter of Samuel Williams and only daughter of William Varco Williams, on 4 October 1956 despite the shipyard experiencing a strike by welders. Specially strengthened for lying on the bottom at low water, she was a repeat of **Hudson Deep**, but some sixty feet longer with a deadweight of 10,000 tonnes on a loaded summer draught of 25' 10.5".

At her handing over in January 1957, Mr A J K Goldsmith commented that when **Hudson Deep** entered service she made a loss on her first voyage of £6,500 due to poor freight rates and this continued when she lost nearly half that amount again on her second voyage. However her builders had expected her to burn 12 tons of oil per day at 12 knots when in actual fact she was consuming 10.3 tons per day at the same speed. Since entering service she had sailed nearly 280,000 miles.

Hudson Point sailed from the Tyne on 18 January for the Thames, sailing on her first transatlantic passage on 24 January for San Pedro de Macoris in the Dominican Republic. Six months after her commissioning **Hudson Point** discharged a cargo of bulk sugar at Dagenham Dock in two days. Had the cargo been carried in bags the discharge would have taken eight days longer. The turn round saved the company an estimated £3,000. While the company now owned two large deep-sea motorships its steamers were also venturing further afield than the collier trade. In July 1957, **Hudson Sound** (1) loaded timber in the Siberian port of Igarka for Aberdeen and then began a CEA charter before loading pitch at Port Clarence on the Tees for Sète in southern France. From there she went to Algeria to load esparto grass for Granton on the Firth of Forth. In April 1958 under the command of Captain Bennet she loaded china clay in Fowey for Montreal. Upon discharge she commenced a charter loading copper concentrates at Tilt Cove, Newfoundland, for Quebec. On completion of this charter in November, she returned to the United Kingdom and in 1959 she returned to Canada for a similar charter.

On 29 June 1957, **Hudson Firth** was outward bound from London to Kingston, Jamaica, with a cargo of cement when she was in collision in thick fog with Royal Mail Lines Ltd's **Loch Ryan** (9935grt/43) 3.5 miles off Start Point. **Loch Ryan**, bound for Hamburg from Vancouver, suffered flooding in her No 2 hold although she was able to make Plymouth that evening under her own power and was surveyed the following day. **Hudson Firth** reported that she was not making water although she could not use her anchors due to bow damage. Arriving at Falmouth that evening, a survey found that she required 29 shell plates repaired around her bow. A temporary collision bulkhead was constructed and she was fitted with temporary anchor fittings before she proceeded to London to discharge her cargo and then Hull for repairs. The incident was deemed as "radar assisted", both ships watching the other's approach on radar and not taking appropriate avoiding action.

Hudson Bank was sold to German owners in 1959 who replaced her steam engine with a diesel engine. As a motorship she only saw service for another six years, foundering off the coast of Sweden in 1965. From 1957 Hudson Steamship had been able to secure summer charters in Canada for several of its ships. **Hudson Sound** (1) spent the summers of 1957 and 1958 loading copper concentrates in Gaspe, Quebec, for Newfoundland, reverting to the north east coast in winter. 1959 and 1960 saw **Hudson Firth** loading general cargo in Canadian east coast ports for the West Indies back loading sugar to Canada. Usually a positioning cargo of china clay from Cornwall was carried across the Atlantic with return cargoes of liner board or forestry products for the UK.

Hudson Bank

(W H Brown, WSPL)

Arthur Lawrence Williams was replaced as Chairman by Lindsay Simpson in 1959 while the previous year Mr W J Crafter had retired as Secretary and Director. He was succeeded as Company Secretary by Mr Albert Cosmo 'Michael' Hamilton. Because Hudson Steamship was now a wholly-owned subsidiary of John Hudson Fuel & Shipping Ltd, there was no need for a full board of individual directors. Its board therefore comprised Lindsay Simpson and Albert Hamilton as mentioned with only one other director, John Carmichael. The other seven directors still controlled the company as they sat on the board of John Hudson Fuel & Shipping Ltd.

THE WILLIAMS HUDSON GROUP : 1960 TO 1968

On 10 December 1962, Samuel Williams & Sons Ltd was restyled Williams Hudson Ltd and became the holding company for John Hudson Fuel & Shipping and Hudson Steamship Co Ltd although the group relationship between the two companies remained unchanged. In time Williams Hudson Ltd became the holding company for other companies which the Williams Hudson Group acquired. At the same time the outstanding equity in John Hudson & Co Ltd was purchased from minority shareholders. In the 1950s, two fuel distribution companies had been acquired which were operated as subsidiaries of John Hudson & Co Ltd, one in Birmingham and one in Glasgow. These two firms now became wholly owned subsidiaries of Williams Hudson Ltd. John Hudson & Co Ltd was also at this time main agents for Gulf Oil (Great Britain) Ltd using Dagenham as its main depot with over 200,000 tons of tank storage capacity.

On 1 April 1964, Mr Arthur Lawrence Williams retired as Executive Chairman of the Williams Hudson Group. He was the last member of the Williams family to head the Group and was succeeded by Mr Lindsay Simpson. In March 1964 John Hudson Fuel & Shipping Ltd was converted to a private company.

While Hudson Steamship's parent group had intended the company to diversify away from the collier trade, the beginning of the 1960s saw a return to that trade. In 1963, **Hudson Deep** (1) was chartered by the Central Electricity Generating Board for a series of experimental cargoes for the Thames. At that time the largest colliers were only 4200 dwt and the CEGB was interested in larger ships for the trade. Although she was returning to the trade that had been the cornerstone of the company's work, she had traded much further afield. Upon completion she had been on charter to Tate & Lyle who eventually replaced her, and other chartered ships, with their own bulk carriers. As a result **Hudson Deep** (1) was employed in the North American tramping trades although she obtained some profitable charters carrying iron ore with the Canadian company DOSCO. In January 1960, she loaded coke in Nordenham for Noumea, New Caledonia, and after discharge traded between New Caledonia and Australia with bulk cargoes such as nickel ore, coal and coke. In April 1961 she loaded sugar in Queensland for Dagenham and arrived in the United Kingdom in June 1961.

At this time John Hudson & Co Ltd in conjunction with the Central Electricity Generating Board conceived the idea of using one of the Group's deepsea bulk carriers as a collier capable of loading 7,500 tons. Using a ship of this size created problems in both loading and discharging and a series of trials devised by the Regional Fuel Supplies Officer of the CEGB (Southern Region), John Hudson & Co Ltd and Hudson Steamship produced encouraging results.

On 23 May 1963, **Hudson Deep** (1) loaded 7,500 tons of coal at Sunderland in 18.5 hours. The following week at Blyth she loaded 7,285 tons in less than twelve hours. In her first three trips, **Hudson Deep** (1) delivered 22,000 tons of cargo in thirteen days which represented an average of 1,700 tons per day compared with a figure of 580 tons per day for a 4,500 tonne deadweight collier. As a result the Board negotiated charters with Hudson Steamship, Stephenson Clarke, William Cory and France Fenwick for six single deck 7,000 deadweight colliers. All six were built in the North East. France Fenwick had two built at Bartrams on the Wear while Cory placed an order for one with Blyth Dry Dock & Shipbuilding Co Ltd, who also built two for Stephenson Clarke. After receiving tenders from several yards Hudson Steamship returned to Readheads for a single ship order, the contract being signed on 23 November 1964.

In the meantime, the company sold **Hudson Bay** which had been laid up at Blyth since the latter end of 1963, her buyers being Hughes Bolckow Ltd who broke her up at their yard at Blyth in March 1964. The newbuilding from Redheads was launched on 5 April 1965 as **Hudson Light** by Mrs Lindsay Simpson and was the first collier built on the River Tyne since the end of the Second World War and also the largest. A four hatch collier, she was powered by a Doxford diesel which achieved 14.8 knots on her loaded trials. She was also fitted with a bow thrust unit. She had been designed with help from the Yarrow Admiralty Research Department, Scotstoun. Her Erman hatch covers, built under licence by MacGregors, were, in section, like a chain of truncated cones which rolled up, one inside the other. This box shape gave her the strength to carry a deck cargo if required.

*The **Hudson Light** leaves the locks at Brunsbüttel and heads into the River Elbe on 24 June 1971.*

(Malcolm Cranfield)

Her hatch/hold design enabled her to be discharged without the aid of calfdozers and her hatch covers and their dogging arrangements enabled her hatch openings to be wider than the other colliers building at that time. She also suffered less grab damage during discharge, grabs being able to plumb a greater area of the tanktop. With a bunker capacity of 184 tons she could be traded deepsea. When completed, *Hudson Light* was not granted unconditional 100A1 classification by Lloyd's Register. Her engine was a four cylinder 'P' type Doxford diesel which was the first to be fitted with a variable pitch propeller. When operated with her bow thruster, the propulsion system gave excellent manoeuvrability but suffered from torsional vibration problems. Lloyd's Register requested that it be inspected after three months service and during the first inspection it was found that the internal absorption springs had broken. As a result, the vessel continued in service with a claused classification for some time and in the ensuing years became a floating testbed for the Doxford design team. The problem resulted in operating losses for the ship until it was learned from Lloyd's Register that the Royal Fleet Auxiliary ships *Hebe* and *Bacchus* had conquered a similar problem by fitting a Holset rubber coupling. In the case of *Hudson Light* this was overcome by the fitting of two standard units back to back in the engine's drive train and was the biggest marine application of this type. As a result of this correction, *Hudson Light* was eventually granted 100 A1 classification.

Hudson Light was two months late into service due to a shortage of skilled labour at the shipyard. At her handing over Mr Lindsay Simpson made no apologies for the comments he had made at the company's AGM prior to her completion when he estimated that the ship had lost £40,000 in earnings due to the delay. Her acceptance trials took place on 30 July, the vessel running a series of trials in a light condition. She then loaded 6,770 tons of coal at Harton Staithes, South Shields before running loaded trials. On completion of these trials she began a seven-year charter to CEGB. With the entry into service of the six new colliers between October 1964 and February 1967 the older steam colliers were disposed of from the CEGB and chartered fleets. After *Hudson Deep* (1) was returned to the company, a long-term charter was obtained for her with the Colonial Sugar Refining Co, Sydney, for the carriage of bulk sugar. In 1966 *Hudson Light* was transferred to the ownership of John Hudson Fuel & Shipping Ltd and she was the first ship to be owned by them and they became the principal shipowning arm of the Williams Hudson Group with future acquisitions being registered under their ownership. The existing fleet remained under the ownership of Hudson Steamship. New tonnage, although registered under the ownership of John Hudson Fuel & Shipping Ltd, was operated by Hudson Steamship.

Until 1966, J W Dale & Sons Ltd had provided Hudson Steamship with a full superintendency for their ships; Hudsons only had a small number of office staff engaged in chartering and fixing cargo. Dale & Sons were responsible for technical matters, crews and ship's running costs. However in 1966 it was decided to end this arrangement as Dale had recommended the replacing of *Hudson River*'s tanktops during a drydocking. The cost of this was £40,000, a sum in excess of the vessel's value and the group decided to terminate their arrangement with Dale. Hudson Steamship now began to manage their own ships and office staff were now employed to manage the day to day running of the fleet.

By 1966, the Williams Hudson Group's profits were decreasing. When the Group had expanded capital had been raised by issuing debentures to the Prudential Insurance Company secured on Group assets. The result was that all the Group's assets were subject to the provisions of the debenture trust deed. In order to improve cash flow and bolster Group profits it was decided to sell several ships in the fleet that were not on charter. The first ship to be sold was *Hudson Cape* and she was handed over on 12 September to Cypriot owners after a sale drydocking at Tyne Dock Engineering Ltd, South Shields. Her new owners intended to trade her in the Mediterranean and she was converted to oil fired machinery. *Hudson Cape* had spent most of her career on time charter to John Hudson & Co Ltd or to the Continent with coal and sugar.

Hudson Cape

(W H Brown, WSPL)

Although she had spent a virtually trouble-free career with the company, *Hudson Cape* came close to ending her service earlier than she actually did. On 21 December 1962, she was anchored in the Halfway Reach opposite the Thunderer jetty waiting to discharge coal from Blyth. At 0645 she was struck by the tanker *Allurity*, owned by F T Everard & Sons Ltd, which was inward for the Royal Docks with fuel oil. The tanker suffered steering gear failure and hit *Hudson Cape* on her starboard quarter, above and below the waterline. *Hudson Cape* was beached between the Thunderer and No 4 jetty at Dagenham, assisted by the tugs *Sun XVII*, *Sun XIV*, *Challenge*, *Muria*, *Danube VIII* and *Arthur* with the operation supervised by the Port of London Salvage Department. *Hudson Cape* suffered flooding to her engine and boiler rooms and her accommodation block at high water. No 4 hold was also flooded due to either the failure or leakage in her cross bunker forward bulkhead. *Allurity* suffered a small hole on her port bow and a bent stem. She was able to berth at the Royal Albert Dock and was later surveyed at her owner's yard at Greenhithe.

Hudson Steamship anticipated that the vessel would be abandoned to her insurers given her age and possibly the fact that the group were in negotiations with the Central Electricity Generating Board about the introduction of larger tonnage. However the Group's Engineering Department at Dagenham were able to weld a plate over the area of the damaged hull and pump out the water in her engine room. On 23 December, *Hudson Cape* was refloated using Port of London lifting craft and was berthed alongside the No 7 Jetty at Dagenham to discharge her 3,000 tons of coal, completed on the next day. *Hudson Cape* was later towed to the Tyne for repairs before she was able to re-enter service the following year.

After only nine years service, *Hudson Point* was sold in November 1966 to Hong Kong owners for £325,000 and was handed over at the Fujinagata Dockyard, Osaka, on 12 December having arrived on 6 December from Newcastle, New South Wales, via Port Kembla. After delivery from her builders, she had spent two years on charter to Tate & Lyle loading sugar in the Caribbean with most of her cargoes being discharged at Dagenham. *Hudson Point* had been displaced from the West Indies sugar trade in 1958 by Tate & Lyle's own Sugar Line. The previous year, she had loaded coal in Hampton Roads for Europe and was now fixed on single voyage charters and the following is a sample of the work found for her by the company.

In September 1958 she loaded phosphates for Durban, South Africa, backloading sugar for London after discharge. In March 1959 she loaded coal at Hampton Roads for Santos and then sugar in Rio for London. For the rest of the year she went on charter to Federal Commerce and worked in the Great Lakes from April until the end of the season. She returned to Canada in 1960, loading coal in Sydney, Nova Scotia, for Montreal and returned to Rotterdam in November 1960. She returned to the sugar trade in 1961 trading around Australian ports and in March and April 1962 was trading around British Columbia.

Hudson Point briefly returned to the sugar trade when she was chartered by L M Fischel & Co Ltd, London in April 1962 to carry Cuban sugar to the UK, the freight rate being 50s 6d (£2.52) per ton. After discharging at Liverpool, she sailed in ballast on a time charter of $800 per day for Hampton Roads to load coal for Pasajes for a Spanish firm, Compania General Carbones S.A., Madrid. June 1963 saw her sailing from Mackay for Auckland, New Zealand, when she was fixed for coal from Adelaide to Noumea, New Caledonia, on behalf of a French company, Le Nickel S A, Paris. The company received a lump sum payment of £8,800 for this cargo and after discharging she loaded iron ore in Prony Bay, New Caledonia, for The Broken Hill Pty Co Ltd. Compared to the freight rate for her Cuban sugar in 1962 the freight rate was only 14s (70p) per ton. Towards the end of 1963, she was fixed for a cargo of sugar from Pointe des Galets, Réunion Island, in the Indian Ocean to Auckland for the Colonial Sugar Refining Co Ltd, Sydney, who later took *Hudson Deep* on long term charter. It is interesting to note that for this charter the freight rate depended on the amount of cargo carried, which was at the master's option. If the vessel carried between 9000 to 9450 metric tons of cargo the freight rate was 117s 6d (£5.77) per ton but if she carried 10,000 to 10,500 the rate dipped to 110s (£5.50) per ton.

In 1964 and 1965, *Hudson Point* continued to carry sugar and iron ore in Australia and the Far East. October 1964 saw her on another Broken Hill charter, loading iron ore at Cockatoo Island in Yampi Sound, Western Australia, for Newcastle NSW. After discharging, she loaded coal at Newcastle for a Japanese port in the Moji Chiba range for Nissho & Co Ltd, Tokyo. In the details for her various charters, she is fixed to load no less than 9,500 tons and no more than 10,500 tons of cargo. For the coal to Japan she was expected to load at the average rate of no less than 4,000 tons per day. During this time *Hudson Point* also visited the ports of Penang and Chittagong, both far removed from the company's east coast collier trade.

In July 1965, she loaded pyrites at Foynes, Eire, for Brownsville, Texas, and was then fixed with The National Sulphuric Acid Association Ltd, London, for a return cargo of sulphur from Beaumont, Texas, to Manchester where she was one of the largest ships able to use the Manchester Ship Canal locks. With a beam of 61' she just fitted into the Canal locks which were 64' in width. Freight was 70s per ton with loading to average 3,000 tons per day in Beaumont, but discharge was to average only 1,500 tons per day in Manchester. She again loaded pyrites at Foynes for New Orleans, returning to Manchester with sulphur. Ballasting to Bremen she then loaded potash for Baltimore and Richmond, Virginia. Upon completion she loaded coal at Newport News for Aviles in Spain, arriving there towards the end of January 1966.

In 1967, *Hudson Strait* and *Hudson Firth*, together with the smaller *Hudson Sound* (1), were sold to Panamanian owners. *Hudson Strait* was sold for £25,200 and was handed over to her new owners on the Thames at Denton Tier on 5 January 1967. *Hudson Firth* was taken over at Dagenham on 21 February 1967, her sale realising £55,000. Under the command of Captain Tait in 1966, *Hudson Firth* had featured in a BBC Schools Broadcast on the Home Service. Carrying a reporter on a regular voyage from Blyth to Dagenham, the resulting programme was part of a geography series. The company had lately found cargoes for her away from the collier trade, loading steel in UK for

Spain from July until September 1965 and in the spring and early summer of 1966 she loaded potash in Germany for the USA with return cargoes of paper from Canada.

Hudson Sound (1) was sold on 13 March 1967 for £46,000 although the price had originally been £49,000. In the last two months of 1963, she was employed on a time charter in European waters, followed by a spell on the east coast until May 1964 when she was fixed on a six month time charter carrying copper concentrates on the Canadian east coast. She returned to the collier trade until May 1966 when she went back to Canada for another time charter until November. At the end of that charter she was employed on the east coast for only a month and was laid up from Christmas Day 1966 until 21 February 1967. Coming out of lay-up, she traded for only three weeks for CEGB because the company had agreed her sale while laid up.

*A three-quarter stern view of the **Hudson Firth** outward bound in ballast from the River Thames.*

(A Duncan, WSPL)

Hudson Sound

(WSPL)

The sale of the fleet also meant a cutback in crew who were no longer required. Many of the crews, especially the masters, had been with the company for many years and this is an appropriate point to mention them. Masters made redundant at this time included Captain F Wickman, regular master of **Hudson Strait** and before her **Dagenham**, who was also certified to command square rigged sailing ships. Captain Wickman along with the previously-mentioned Captain Tait both became North Sea pilots. There was also Captain James Gibbons DSC and Captain Bill Munday who between them commanded **Hudson Deep** (1) and **Hudson Sound** (1). Both came back at later dates as relief masters, Captain Gibbons returned to his native Whitehaven and was employed as a hospital laundry Superintendent although he returned as relief master on **Hudson Light** for a time. Captain Munday eventually became a cargo surveyor based in Sunderland. While the company lost experienced collier captains, it still retained a pool of competent masters and crew although there were many comings and goings. From the late 1950s through to the late 1980s, there were two masters, Captain Willey and Captain Horsley, who both remained with the company for over thirty years serving in the majority of the owned and managed vessels.

The three steamers continued in service for their new owners into the early 1970s with **Hudson Point** trading until 1979. With these sales the fleet now stood at three ships, **Hudson Deep** (1) trading mainly in the Australian sugar trade while **Hudson Light** and **Hudson River** were employed in the coal trade.

THE WILLIAMS HUDSON GROUP : 1968 TO 1972

Because of falling profits, Hudson Steamship could not afford to purchase new tonnage from finances within the Group. With the introduction of investment grants however, initially 25% and then a further 20%, there was a possibility for purchase given that subsequent employment could be found. The legislation introducing the investment grants required that the asset be British owned and operated for a minimum of five years and any charters obtained be at the market rate. With up to 80% finance being available on a newbuilding there now existed an opportunity for the company to purchase newly-built tonnage.

An immediate replacement for **Hudson Point** was found in 1968 when a 23,400dwt bulk carrier was purchased for £2.2 million from Norwegian owner Georg Vefling. At the time of her purchase she was still fitting out at her builder's yard in Tønsberg, having been launched as **Belveni**. Veflings had secured an eight year individual voyage charter with Volkswagen for the shipment of cars from Europe to America. Although having the appearance of a conventional bulk carrier, she was fitted with collapsible decks to carry cars. On completion of a car carrying voyage these would be stowed and the ship became a conventional bulk carrier. The charter meant the ship had an outward cargo from Europe to America, provided Volkswagen had cars for shipment. Once the cars had been discharged, it was the operator's responsibility to find a return cargo to Europe.

As a result, John Hudson Fuel & Shipping Ltd and Hudson Steamship became nominal owners of **Bel-Hudson**, the new name for the vessel, with Veflings having overall control of the vessel. The Norwegian Government was happy with this arrangement as long as there was an 80% Norwegian involvement. To avoid negative cash flow the vessel had to be earning all the time, even while off charter. To compensate for this it was agreed that Veflings would be offered an option to purchase after five years at a predetermined price. This was based on the book written down value since the depreciation was funded by the original purchaser, i e Veflings. Finance for the purchase of **Belveni** came from a mortgage of $2.61 million from Hambro Bank and two mortgages from Norwegian principles. These were NKr 7.48 million from Atkieselskapet Laneinstituttet, on behalf of Skipsbyggeriene, and NKr 3.74 million from Bohn & Co Ltd.

This arrangement saw the Williams Hudson Group benefit by having Hudson Steamship earnings increase through management fees and positive cash flow through profitable charters. The latter was bolstered by a substantial depreciation element as well as 100% tax free depreciation available for the Group's tax relief. The deal between Williams Hudson and Vefling was handled by P G Mender, Vefling's financial advisor, and as a result of the mutual trust between the two companies other similar deals were forthcoming. Her renaming reflected the agreement between Vefling and Hudson. Veflings named their ships with the prefix Bel with Hudson marking the involvement of Williams Hudson. When completed, **Bel-Hudson**, bore the funnel markings of Georg Vefling.

*A splendid view of the **Bel-Hudson** underway and fully laden.*

(Dag Bakka jr)

Bel-Hudson ran trials in Oslo Fjord on 15 August 1968 and then sailed to Hamburg where she was fitted with her collapsible car decks by Blohm & Voss. She was handed over to the company on 10 October 1968 at Hamburg and sailed for Bremen arriving there on the next day. She loaded a total of 1,806 assorted Volkswagen cars, of which 1,306 were for Los Angeles, the balance for Vancouver. She sailed on the morning of Sunday 12 October under the command of Captain H M Horsley and arrived at Cristobal at the northern end of the Panama Canal on 28 October. Passage through the canal took nine hours and on clearing she took a further seven days to Los Angeles. At Los Angeles she berthed directly under a newly-constructed suspension bridge. The dockers refused to unload her fearing they might be hit by a falling object from the bridge. As a result she was moved some six hundred feet up the quay before unloading started. She sailed on Friday 8 October for Vancouver, arriving three days later to finish discharge. A cargo of grain had been fixed for Holland and she sailed from Vancouver on 18 November. On arrival at Amsterdam, where she discharged at the Vlothaven Granary, she was only six hours over her expected time of arrival due to bad weather during the last 72 hours of her passage. On her second voyage she took cars to Vancouver and then loaded timber for United States eastern seaboard ports, discharging at Puerto Rico, Newhaven, Connecticut, Brooklyn and Camden, New Jersey before loading coal for Hamburg.

Return cargoes for **Bel-Hudson** were either coal from Hampton Roads or grain from the Great Lakes, her cargoes being fixed by Vefling through another Norwegian company, A/S Platon, Oslo. **Bel-Hudson** was the first of some sixty bulk carriers chartered to Volkswagen for one-way car carrying. In 1969 **Bel-Hudson** made her first passage to the Great Lakes. With 1,836 cars she sailed from Emden passing through the Pentland Firth for the Great Lakes. She passed inspection for entry into the St Lawrence Seaway where the maximum permitted width was 75ft 6ins, **Bel-Hudson**'s beam being 75' 2". A mostly daylight passage took her into Lake Ontario and she then transited the Welland Canal to Lake Erie, negotiating eight locks and being lifted 327 feet in the process. On entering Lake Erie she berthed at Toledo to discharge what was the largest single car shipment at that time. Completing discharge she sailed to Chicago to load grain for Brake. Transiting back through the Lakes, she topped up her cargo at Montreal. Ships were refused entry into the locks if their draught exceeded 25' 9" and **Bel-Hudson** could increase her beam by up to six inches if she listed half a degree.

At the 1969 Annual General Meeting, the Group reported that **Hudson Deep** (1) and **Bel-Hudson** had earned in freights the equivalent of £771,321 in dollars and other foreign currency. In 1971 the company agreed a charter for **Hudson Light** to Stora Koppersberg Bergslaga A/B, Falun, Sweden, to carry coke from Germany to Sweden with a return cargo of iron ore at a rate of £565 per day. The vessel went on charter on 1 April 1972, her charterer reputedly being the oldest company in Sweden. For the first two years of her career she had been employed by the CEGB until she was not required, even though she had commenced trading with an seven year charter. She was then time chartered to an Italian company, Henri Coe & Clerici to carry scrap. **Hudson Deep** (1) had returned to the UK from the Pacific in June 1970 after several years on charter to carry sugar from Queensland and Fijian ports to Auckland, New Zealand. That trade had finished in 1970 and she was used to carry coal on behalf of John Hudson & Co Ltd and other fuel distributors. Before her entry into the coal trade, she had her cargo derricks removed to assist discharging.

While trading in the Pacific, **Hudson Deep** (1) had voluntarily undertaken weather reports for the Meteorological Office and in 1968 the company received a letter commending the efforts of her crew. At that time there were around 500 UK registered ships sending in weather reports. The reports submitted by **Hudson Deep** (1) were valuable because the area in which she traded was sparsely covered by shipping. To return to the UK she was fixed with a cargo of urea loaded in Adelaide and was employed for nearly two years on the coast until her sale to Cypriot owners in 1972, her cargo gear being refitted prior to handing over.

On 8 March 1969 while departing Tilbury "B" power station for Immingham, **Hudson Light** was in collision with British India's **Chantala** (7556grt/50) near No 1 Sea Reach Buoy. **Hudson Light** suffered bow damage above her waterline and anchored near No 1 Sea Reach Buoy until noon the following day when she moved upriver for survey at Gravesend Upper Buoy. After survey by the company's superintendents and Lloyd's Register, it was agreed that a small temporary patch be fitted in way of the damage to allow her to proceed up the coast prior to permanent repairs, damage being very local to the point of contact. **Hudson Light** sailed on 11 March for South Shields where she was repaired at Redheads before re-entering service. **Chantala**, on passage from Chittagong to Middlesbrough, was opened up just forward of her bridge, from the sheer strake to her bilges and was drydocked at Tilbury for repairs.

In 1969, the Williams Hudson Group acquired the oil broking company Lambert & Bendall Ltd with a view to entering the international oil market. As a result of this acquisition, the first tanker to be operated by the group was purchased in January 1970 and registered in the ownership of John Hudson Fuel & Shipping Ltd. Built for Norwegian owners Westfal Larsen A/S, Bergen, she was a 19,000 dwt motor tanker completed by J L Thompson Ltd, Sunderland, as **Spinanger**. When John Hudson Fuel & Shipping Ltd bought **Spinanger**, they borrowed $780,000 from Westfal Larsen to purchase the vessel which was not fully repaid until June 1976, well after they resold her for further trading.

It was intended that the tanker, now renamed **Hudson Trader**, would be time chartered to Lambert & Bendall Ltd for carrying clean products as she had been chartered by them on several occasions. However a survey by Hudson Steamship, who were to manage her, found that she was not suitable due to her structural condition. As a result of these findings, a "no off-hire" contract was negotiated whereby Hudson Steamship were paid management fees even if the vessel was not able to trade. This proved to be a wise move as the vessel spent long periods in drydock during her operation. In 1972, for example, she was dry-docked on the Tyne from 4 March until 15 June. While Hudson Steamship benefitted through this "no off-hire" clause, the Williams Hudson Group did not as Lambert & Bendall had to pay for her hire which was tied to her running costs so that the extra repair bills did not fall to Hudson Steamship. The associated group company John Hudson & Co Ltd awarded a contract to John Hudson Fuel & Shipping Ltd for the operation of a specialised effluent carrier to carry inert blended chemicals. The order was placed with Dutch builders at a contract price of £450,000. Williams Hudson companies would look after the whole process of disposal, John Hudson & Co Ltd had a fleet of road tankers which would transport the waste to storage tanks situated at Dagenham and John Hudson Fuel & Shipping Ltd would dispose of the waste at sea.

The ship was launched on 11 December 1970 as **Hudson Stream** by Mrs B A Whittet, wife of John Hudson & Co Ltd's Managing Director. Designed for the transportation of approved liquid waste products for disposal at sea, she was able to work in shallow waters and load cargo when aground. An area of approximately seventy five square miles to the seaward of the Kentish Knock was allocated by the Ministry of Agriculture and Fisheries for the dumping of waste. Disposal of the waste was to take place at about six feet below the surface with the vessel steaming at her maximum speed of 12.5 knots. Cargo capacity was 1,500 tons, with a maximum discharge rate of 300 tons per hour.

When completed, **Hudson Stream** was immediately laid up at Dagenham Dock. The contract for which she had been ordered had been cancelled due to environmental fears voiced by the Norwegian Government. They believed the effluent waste would be carried by tides to the Norwegian coast and she never traded for the company although they still benefitted as they had negotiated a "no off-hire" contract similar to the one drawn up for **Hudson Trader**. **Hudson Stream** was sold in 1972, renamed **Bowstream** and converted to a sand dredger. Shortly after her sale she was in collision with a Dutch inland waterways barge in the Oude Maas and after her salvage was extensively rebuilt before returning to trade.

*Photographs of the **Hudson Stream** are extremely rare. This view was taken in the shipyard on the day of her launch.*

(John Appleby)

Even rarer are views of the ship underway. This photograph was taken when the tanker was on trials.
(A Vuyk & Zonen's Scheepsbouwwerven NV, courtesy Bert Kruidhof))

In November 1971, both John Hudson Fuel & Shipping Ltd and Hudson Steamship Co Ltd moved from their offices in London to 36 Ship Street, Brighton, above Williams & Glynn Bank. It had been decided to sell the London offices to raise finances for further group expansion. Hudson Steamship continued managing the fleet which remained owned by John Hudson Fuel & Shipping Ltd. In 1971, **Hudson River** was converted to burn oil as it was now difficult to buy suitable bunker coal and this led to reduced crewing costs as less crew were required. In 1968 the company had decided to sell her for scrap but circumstances had led to a further two years of profitable trading from the north east to Dagenham on charter to the CEGB and the company made more money than they would have done if she had been broken up. In July 1970, the company secured a charter for her carrying coal from Szczecin, Poland, to power stations in Hamburg. After this, work became hard to find for her and she was laid up at Blyth before her sale to Panamanian owners in 1973.

At the beginning of 1970, the Williams Hudson Group were approached by A/S Noralliance, Oslo, a consortium of Norwegian tanker owners, to operate on their behalf two steam VLCCs ordered from Swedish shipbuilders Kockums Mekaniska Verkstads AB, Malmö. Noralliance was a joint venture company formed by Odd Berg, Hjalmar Bjørge, Erling H Samuelsen, P Meyer and Olsen & Ugelstad. All these partners were tanker operators but could not agree which company should manage the ships. Because of his dealings with Williams Hudson in respect of **Bel-Hudson**, it was Per Mender, who was also Noralliance's lawyer and who was aware of the British Government's Investment Grant scheme, who suggested John Hudson Fuel & Shipping as operators of the vessels. A/S Noralliance had ordered the two ships for trading between Europe and the Middle East and after six months negotiations the contracts were transferred to John Hudson Fuel & Shipping Ltd with Hudson Steamship as the ships' managers.

The management arrangement for the two VLCCs was similar to that of **Bel-Hudson** with the nominal ownership and management with the Williams Hudson Group through John Hudson Fuel & Shipping Ltd and Hudson Steamship. The funding for the construction of the vessels, £19 million for the pair, came from the British Government's Investment Grant for British shipowners. Introduced in the 1960s it initially provided 25% of the contract building price paid in stages up to delivery. At the time it was normal for the shipowner to obtain an 80% loan under the Government's Guaranteed Finance Scheme. In practice a British shipowner could order a newbuilding without having to put up any of his money. This grant was the reason why so many foreign shipowners set up British subsidiaries in the 1960s. Both ships were designed with a deadweight of 254,500 tons and were powered by steam turbines giving a speed of 15.5 knots. Turbine cargo pumps with a capacity of 3,500 tons per hour gave a loading/discharging time of around sixteen hours while all fifteen cargo tanks were fitted with an inert gas system to maintain non-explosive conditions. The vessels were both fitted with a radar docking system enabling a controlled rate of approach to any berth.

They were also fitted with three independent radar anti-collision devices, one of which was capable of tracking targets and fulfilling normal anti-collision functions automatically. Accommodation was to a high standard, all crew having single cabins and leisure facilities included a swimming pool, gymnasium, sauna, cinema and bar. A lift in the accommodation gave access to all six decks, which were air conditioned and heated throughout. The safety and complicated equipment on board these vessels meant that a specialist consultant company was employed for the training of crews. At the time of their completion they were the largest vessels under the British flag. As there was a shortage of experienced VLCC tanker officers, the company had to recruit personnel from established tanker companies and in order to attract the right personnel offered a higher rate of pay than other operators.

Hudson Venture

(M Cassar, WSPL)

The first to be completed was named **Hudson Venture** and was floated out of her building dock on 25 April 1971. She was christened on 14 May by Mrs Lars Krogh and handed over in June 1971. She was time chartered to A/S Noralliance, Oslo, who sub-chartered her for three years to Texaco (Panama) Inc, Panama, and operated from the Persian Gulf to the UK and Europe. Her sister, **Hudson Friendship**, was handed over in September 1971. Also chartered to A/S Noralliance, she was sub-chartered to Gulf Oil, Pennsylvania, and operated between the Persian Gulf and North America as well as the UK, Europe and the Far East.

The maiden voyage of **Hudson Venture** illustrated the differences in operating large supertankers compared to coastal colliers. **Hudson Venture** part-loaded her first cargo in Iran at Kharg Island and the balance at Ras Tanura, Saudi Arabia. The first port of discharge was to be Milford Haven with the remaining 110,000 tons for Zeebrugge which Hudsons were unhappy about because of the position of the tanker berth at Zeebrugge. On entry the ship would have to make a sharp 70 degree turn, with only a ship's length to take the way off the ship. At that time the tugs available were too small and underpowered to handle a ship the size of **Hudson Venture**. She berthed in Zeebrugge on 28 August 1971 although coming alongside she was beam on to the prevailing wind. Once alongside her problems continued. Her cooling system became choked by small crabs sucked into the condensers resulting in the cooling system being shut down and having to be cleaned before steam was raised again.

On this occasion her discharge took nearly a week, while under normal conditions it should have been eighteen hours. Her crew bought a fishing net to protect the intakes with some success and they later found out that before the berth had been built the area was a breeding ground for crabs. While leaving Zeebrugge on 28 August, **Hudson Venture** suffered a loss of power and required the attending tugs to tow her to a safe anchorage some ten miles off the coast. While at anchor she suffered a boiler explosion and went to Rotterdam for repairs until 25 September.

At the time of the tankers' completion, Hudson Steamship was paid $240,000 per annum per vessel in management fees. This was based on a dollar conversion rate of $2.40 giving a fee of £100,000. Soon after this fee was fixed there was a sterling crisis and the rate went up to $2.70. Hudson Steamship asked for the fee to be renegotiated but Noralliance refused and soon after the dollar fell to around $1.70 putting Hudsons in a better financial state. Both vessels were each fixed on six-year charters with a "no off-hire" agreement. In 1973, Hudson Steamship was awarded the management of a 116,000dwt bulk carrier building in Uddevalla, Sweden. Completed in December 1973 as **Varangfjell**, her owners were Townsend Car Ferries Ltd, a company more associated with cross-Channel ferries. The reasons Townsend branched into bulk carriers were purely financial and they obtained a time charter for her with A/S Luksefjell & A/S Rudolf, a subsidiary of Olsen & Ugelstad, one of the partners in A/S Noralliance. They in turn placed the vessel under the management of Hudson Steamship because of their dealing with the two VLCCs. **Varangfjell** was named in the style of Olsen & Ugelstad whose vessels' names all ended in "fjell", and throughout her charter carried this company's funnel markings.

Hudson Trader *was sold to Greek owners in June 1973. Most of her trading had been in the Mediterranean with occasional cargoes loaded in the West Indies. Her final voyage for the company was from Aruba to Cardiff from where she ballasted to Barry and there she was handed over to her new owners.*

(Captain D Wiley)

*Photographed on 17 September 1971, the **Hudson Friendship** is thought to be on her delivery voyage when this fine image was taken.*

(Company archives)

TAKEOVER OF THE WILLIAMS HUDSON GROUP : 1971

The success of John Hudson Fuel & Shipping Ltd in obtaining the management contracts for the VLCCs and **Bel-Hudson** had led to a revival of the Williams Hudson Group's profits. Its assets had significantly multiplied as apart from the ships the group also owned large areas of land in the UK, at Dagenham, and abroad, mainly in Canada.

In 1960 Samuel Williams (B.C.) Ltd, later restyled British Columbia Wharves Ltd, was formed to control the group's 75% shareholding in Vancouver Wharves Ltd. Vancouver Wharves was situated on a prime 90 acre site in Vancouver with a quay frontage of some 3,000' able to take ships with a draught of up to 35'. It had its own marshalling yards and was able to take up to 250 railcars per day and had the first large wharf side potash shed and first dockside bagging plant in Western Canada. Within three years of the site opening it was handling 1,000,000 tons of exports from British Columbia and in 1966 a new bulk loader capable of loading ships of 70,000 tons at a rate of 4,500 tons per hour was installed. This gave a potential output of 8 million tons per annum compared to 2.5 million tons at 50% berth occupancy. By the late 1960s, land occupied by Vancouver Wharves had grown to 163 acres and was handling in excess of three million tons of minerals, lumber, fertilisers, pulp and paper.

In 1966 the value of the land and buildings at Dagenham was £3.8 million, compared with a figure of £1.8 million in 1961. The net assets of the Group were estimated at £9 million, half this amount being made up of the value of land in the UK and Canada. At the 1967 Annual General Meeting, the group's pre-tax profits were £285,999, compared with the previous year's figure of £472,477. Samuel Williams (B.C.) Ltd later purchased more land at Kitimat with the intention of building fifteen 1000 feet berths to handle bulk cargoes from central British Columbia, Alberta and Saskatchewan. This project was known as Kitimat Wharves Ltd and was a wholly owned subsidiary of Samuel Williams (B.C.) Ltd.

In a joint venture with the proprietors of Hays Wharf Ltd, Williams Hays Holdings was created and in 1965 purchased the Dutch company N.V.Citex Havenbedrijf which owned two large deepwater quays in the port of Rotterdam. A direct subsidiary of the Dutch company was Citex London Ltd, which in turn owned a 50% share in Sheerness Harbour (Stevedore) Ltd which handled the entire warehousing and stevedore operations in Sheerness Harbour.

Viewed from outside, Williams Hudson was seen to be making poor returns from valuable assets. Away from its shipping and fuel distribution companies, it also had an engineering group and its Associated Technology Group, whose two main trading interests were the manufacture and sale of solid lubricants and the design, manufacture and sale of centralised lubrication equipment. The group was the subject of three separate takeovers from outside companies, two of which failed, the third being successful. This bid was orchestrated by David Rowland who had made himself a millionaire through property dealings in the 1960s. Based in Monaco, Rowland bid for the group through a UK-based company which he controlled, Adepton Ltd, offering unsecured loan stock as the consideration. The directors of the Williams Hudson Group saw this offer as a reverse takeover bid on a one-for-ten basis and considered that their shareholders were being offered near worthless stock which in practice would be secured on the assets that Adepton was trying to purchase.

A bitter battle ensued for sixteen weeks with the Williams Hudson Group asking for the take-over to be referred to the Monopolies Commission as they believed the takeover bid breached the Companies Act. Adepton was represented by Williams Brandt Ltd at the hearings while Morgan Grenfell represented Williams Hudson. The bid made City history and caused a substantial rewriting of City rules concerning mergers and takeovers. In the end Williams Brandt was forced to underwrite the bid made by Adepton Ltd and the directors of the Williams Hudson Group were now presented with a bid that they felt they had to recommend to their shareholders. As a result of Williams Brandt having to underwrite the bid they lost their financial independence, in time becoming a subsidiary of one of their major shareholders.

At the same time that Williams Hudson Group Ltd was in the process of being taken over, it had negotiated the purchase of Carless Capel & Leonard Ltd for £1.5 million. This offer was dependant on Carless securing a contract for the purchase of North Sea gas condensate. Because of the bid from Adepton, the purchase of Carless Capel & Leonard could not take place without Adepton's permission, which was refused as the offer would deplete cash and increase profit forecasts. As a result of the takeover, Mr Lindsay Simpson resigned as Executive Chairman of the Williams Hudson Group on 30 September 1970, as did the Deputy Group Chairman Mr Alec Clark-Kennedy. On 8 November 1971, Mr A C Hamilton was replaced as Hudson Steamship's Secretary by Mr Ian Patrick Hicks although Mr Hamilton remained with the group until he retired in 1975.

DECLINE OF THE WILLIAMS HUDSON GROUP : 1972 TO 1977

The offer made to the group's shareholders in the take-over resulted in Adepton Ltd being saddled with large debts which had to be met from the group's resources. Unfortunately the land owned by Williams Hudson Group Ltd was let on long term leases and could not be sold to realise its value. A similar situation existed with the ships on long term charters. As a result the group's credibility suffered and prevented the possibility of further ship management contracts as the Norwegians were unsure of the group's new management. Having opposed the takeover, Hudson Steamship's Managing Director, Mr A K Reynolds, offered to buy the company from Adepton Ltd after gaining support from within A/S Noralliance but this offer was refused. Mr Reynolds resigned from his directorships within the group on 30 May 1972 and was succeeded as Managing Director of Hudson Steamship by Mr J E Appleby who had been with the Hudson Steamship Co Ltd since 1947.

On 30 April 1973, John Hudson Fuel & Shipping Ltd signed contracts with Cammell Laird Shipbuilders Ltd, Birkenhead, for the construction of four STAT 32 type tankers. The design had been developed by the yard, the name coming from STAndard Tanker of 32,000 dwt, and the ships were intended for worldwide trading. Powered by two Crossley Pielstick engines, they had twenty-four cargo tanks, comprising eight centre tanks with two wing tanks each. The cost of the order was estimated in the region of £20 million with the first ship to be delivered in the middle of 1975. To meet the building costs, John Hudson Fuel & Shipping Ltd took out loans with two banks. In September 1973, they agreed two loans of £4,356,160 with Williams & Glyn Bank for the ships allocated as yard numbers 1365 and 1366. In October a further two loans each worth £4,296,160 were secured with Barclays Bank Ltd for the first two ships, Yard Numbers 1362 and 1363. At the time of the signing of the contracts, Cammell Laird was desperate for work and the contract was seen as the yard's saviour.

The first ship of the order, yard number 1362, was launched on 12 February 1975 as **Hudson Progress**, with the second, **Hudson Cavalier**, launched on 24 July 1975. **Hudson Progress** ran her acceptance trials in July 1975 and on completion of these trials was laid up on the Mersey. During the period between placing the order and the first launch, the Yom Kippur War in October 1973 changed trading conditions in the tanker markets. As a result of Egyptian forces crossing the Suez Canal into Israeli territory, tensions ran high because of the region's importance to western economies. The growing political tension in the region resulted in a co-ordinated policy of oil production and prices by the OPEC countries. The periods of cheap fuel were over and most western economies experienced low economic growth coupled with stagnation and long term unemployment. Coupled to the financial instability of the group, John Hudson Fuel & Shipping Ltd was not in a position to accept delivery of the ships.

Hudson Cavalier was completed in December 1976 and was laid up with her sistership. The third ship in the contract, **Hudson Deep** (2), was launched on 22 January 1976 with work on her proceeding at a much slower rate than normal and was not completed until February 1977 and she was laid up without running acceptance trials. It was in December 1976 that the builder and John Hudson Fuel & Shipping Ltd agreed financial terms that enabled repossession of the three tankers. The keel of the fourth ship, yard number 1366, was laid in February 1976, Hudsons allocating the name **Hudson Sound** (2) for her. What little work had been done on the slipway was removed to storage along with other items such as engines ordered by the yard. After the repossession had been completed the yard announced that they would be able to offer her in a completed state at a discounted price to a future owner.

The cancellation of the tankers created severe financial pressures on John Hudson Fuel & Shipping Ltd. Their accounts to 31 March 1976 showed they had paid Cammell Laird £1.86 million in cash instalments for ships whose delivery they had refused. The company made a net trading loss of £1.35 million to the year ending March 1976 and was also liable for mortgage repayments on **Bel-Hudson**, **Hudson Light**, **Hudson Venture** and **Hudson Friendship**. The balance repayable of the investment grant on the two VLCCs was put at £2.18 million and the total sale value of the fleet was put at £39.2 million.

*The bows of the **Hudson Progress** and **Hudson Cavalier** tower above the quayside of Liverpool's Brocklebank Branch Dock on 8 May 1977.*
(Jim McFaul collection)

The three completed ships were laid up in the Mersey at several locations and registered under the ownership of Cammell Laird through subsidiary companies set up to manage the ships. In December 1978, **Hudson Deep** (2) and **Hudson Cavalier** were sold to civilian owners with charters to the Royal Fleet Auxiliary. **Hudson Deep** (2) was converted by her builders and **Hudson Cavalier** went to the Tyne for conversion at Wallsend. Upon completion they were renamed **Brambleleaf** and **Appleleaf** respectively. **Hudson Progress** was sold in 1979 to a finance company for leasing to Norwegian owners and renamed **Balder London**. In 1984 she was chartered to the Royal Fleet Auxiliary and renamed **Orangeleaf**, having already seen service as a chartered ship in the Falklands conflict alongside her two converted sisterships. Yard number 1366, **Hudson Sound** (2), was re-ordered in 1981 by a finance company and launched on 27 October 1981 as **Bayleaf**, chartered to the Royal Fleet Auxiliary. She ran trials on 20-23 March 1982 and was commissioned into the RFA on 26 March. In 1989 **Appleleaf** was leased for five years to Australia with an option to purchase and renamed **Westralia**. Transferred to the Royal Australian Navy on 9 October 1989, she commissioned at Immingham on 27 September 1989 and arrived at Fremantle on 20 December. At present her three sisters remain in the ownership of the Royal Fleet Auxiliary.

The **Appleleaf** was photographed at Portsmouth on 24 July 1983.

(Roy Cressey)

As mentioned, all of the Cammell Laird built ships saw service in the Falklands conflict. On 27 March 1982, **Appleleaf** was ordered to Gibraltar to embark stores for the Task Force while on passage from Curaçao to the United Kingdom with a cargo of fuel, sailing later with **HMS Plymouth**. During the conflict she was involved in 125 Refuelling at Sea (RAS) and pump over operations before sailing from the Falklands on 25 July having being involved in operations since 11 April. **Brambleleaf** was on patrol in the Indian Ocean and was detached from her duties there on 5 April, sailing for South Georgia via the Cape of Good Hope. Ordered to rendezvous in the South Georgia area with a group led by the warship **HMS Antrim** she arrived on 22 April. While on passage she encountered severe weather in the Atlantic and suffered bow damage, which led to some of her cargo tanks being contaminated with sea water. During the night 22/23 April she began to transfer her cargo to the tanker **Tidespring** which was halted due to a submarine. It was later decided to return **Brambleleaf** to the United Kingdom for repairs and on the journey north she transferred fuel and spares to southbound vessels. She returned later with another group to carry out Refuelling at Sea operations and later made a third tour after hostilities had ceased. **Balder London** was one of ten merchant tankers chartered for service with the Royal Fleet Auxiliary. She was taken up from trade on 6 May 1982 and modified at Portsmouth where she was fitted with RAS gear and deck cargo arrangements. She sailed for the South Atlantic on 12 May and was used as an auxiliary support tanker, transporting cargoes into the war area and transferring them to Royal Fleet Auxiliary tankers for distribution. **Bayleaf** completed for service at Portland where the Fleet Maintenance Group installed her RAS equipment and finished off her store rooms and she sailed south loaded with stores and fuel with **Fort Grange** and **Olna**. Employed as a station support tanker, her second RAS was with the liner **Queen Elizabeth 2** and she entered the Total Exclusion Area around the Falklands four days before the Argentinean surrender. After working around the Falklands following the end of the conflict, she sailed for the UK on 31 August 1982.

The **Bayleaf** is seen at Portsmouth in April 2002.

(WSPL)

At the same time that the orders for the four tankers were cancelled, it was decided to sell **Bel-Hudson** and the two VLCCs due to the prevailing economic climate. The middle 1970s had seen a sharp rise in the price of oil and cargoes were hard to secure. Countries in western Europe and the USA were forced to pay high prices to the Middle East oil producing countries and as a result their economies shrank, causing a drop in the demand for oil. In 1976, **Hudson Friendship** and **Hudson Venture** were sold in an en bloc deal to associates of Norwegian ship owner Hilmar Reksten, who operated a fleet of VLCCs, and had taken over A/S Noralliance the previous year. Fortunately for Williams Hudson this deal was concluded some months earlier in 1975 when the value of the ships had been higher, both ships being sold for $50million each. Because of the conditions of the grants which had funded their construction, both ships remained under the British flag and Reksten was not able to own the vessels for some eighteen months. Shortly after the ships were handed over, the VLCC market slumped dramatically. Because of the high price received for the VLCCs John Hudson Fuel & Shipping Ltd was able to pay off the loans against the two tankers. While both vessels were under construction, the company took out four priority mortgages against the value of the ships with a Bermudan company, the Viking Overseas Finance Co Ltd worth $20m for each ship. At the same time as the VLCCs were sold, the company took the opportunity to repay two loans against **Bel-Hudson** and one against **Hudson Light** which had been taken out in July 1974 after the original loan which financed her building had been repaid.

Bel-Hudson was sold for £4.26 million to Oslo-based owners, having traded as a pure bulk carrier since 1975 when her car decks and pontoons had been removed. Her last work as a car carrier had been from Japan to the west coast of the USA in July 1973 for Japan Line Ltd, Tokyo, with return grain cargoes for Japan.

Hudson Light was sold to the Central Electricity Generating Board which left management with Hudson Steamship until 1978. She was one of four chartered colliers which were purchased and she was renamed **Castle Point**, the CEGB's naming policy being that their newer ships were named after headlands between the north-east of England and the Thames. In 1978, she and the other three colliers were transferred to the management of Christian Salvesen Ltd, Leith.

(Russell Priest)

Following these sales, both John Hudson Fuel & Shipping Ltd and Hudson Steamship ceased to be shipowners in their own right, although both companies remained in the Williams Hudson Group as wholly-owned subsidiaries. Mr J Appleby resigned as Hudson Steamship's Managing Director in September 1977 and was replaced by Mr P K Arbuthnot, who had joined the board in 1973 having previously worked for the Newcastle-based shipping company, Common Brothers. In October 1977, the two companies left their offices in Brighton and moved back to London into offices at 8, Maltravers Street, London WC2. Since May 1975, they had been in offices in Academy House, West Street, Brighton, which was formerly the Academy cinema. When this cinema had been demolished and replaced by a purpose office building, John Hudson Fuel & Shipping Ltd took out a long lease on the entire building. Hudson Steamship occupied the 2nd, 3rd and 4th floors while the 1st floor was leased to an insurance company. Up to the time of the relocation to London, the ground floor remained empty but was later taken over by the B.I.C.C. Bank until their worldwide collapse in the late 1980s. The reason for the move was that Williams Hudson had spare space within their offices which could accommodate the two companies.

At about this time, one of the group's subsidiaries, Harrison (London) Ltd, was causing the group trouble, having set up an unauthorised ship management department for the management of two general cargo ships. Harrison's main business was as import, export and shipping agents. They had been active on the Thames for many years as a lighterage company and were acquired by the group in March 1967. The following year, their fleet of tugs and barges was merged with The Dagenham Lighterage Co Ltd, another group company, in a rationalisation move. With this merger, the fleet of six tugs and 155 barges operated by Harrisons on the Thames was taken into group ownership. Due to a decrease in the volume of lighterage work in favour of rail and road in the Port of London, the merged company was wound up on 2 October 1970.

In 1968, a Spanish subsidiary, Harrisons Espanola S A, was set up in Madrid to engage in tanker chartering. In 1970 it became part owner in a Spanish company, Naviera de Cargas Pesados S A, Madrid, which was set up initially to operate two heavy lift ships, **Navipeso Uno** and **Navipeso Dos** (both 500grt/70). However **Navipeso Uno** was sold while fitting out to French owners. Harrisons also provided services for Spanish shipowners and acted as buying agents for the Spanish Government shipyards and as Spanish agents for several British companies.

Through their dealings with the Spanish shipyards, they negotiated two building contracts with Sheikh Rashid Bin Said Al Maktoum, Ruler of Dubai, for two 21,000dwt SANTA FE Type 80 cargo ships. Harrisons had intended the two ships would serve on a liner service between Dubai and Europe with Hamburg as the main European port where another Harrison subsidiary, Harrisons Hamburg GmbH, would act as agents. As part of the agreement to manage the vessels, Harrisons were allowed to set up two companies in Dubai, the first involved selling office equipment, the second an office cleaning firm.

Harrisons had not informed the Ruler that building costs were escalating and due to the difficulties now involved with the contracts, Williams Hudson instructed Hudson Steamship to take over the building supervision, management and operation of the ships. Completed as **Jumairah** and **Mishref** in 1976 and 1977 they were employed in worldwide trading under the Panamanian flag.

Ownership of the vessels legally belonged to two single-ship companies, Dubai Maritime Jumairah S A, Panama City, and Dubai Maritime Mishref S A, Panama City. Dubai Maritime Transport Co was itself incorporated in Dubai and although it owned two gas carriers and a landing craft operating in the Arabian Gulf, it did not have a direct connection to the ships. The operation was always referred to as Dubai Maritime Transport Co, but the legal owners were the two one-ship Panama companies. Prior to the ships entering service, it was suggested that they trade under the British flag and some time was spent establishing what changes might be necessary but this did not occur. Later there was another project undertaken, which again came to nothing, to see if the vessels could be transferred to the United Arab Emirates flag. At that time, the United Arab Emirates were not a signatory to IMCO regulations and there would have had to have been a UAE Merchant Shipping Act drawn up to facilitate the flag's acceptance.

In March 1978, the Managing Director of Harrisons and another director resigned and Mr Arbuthnot took over as Managing Director of Harrisons and their subsidiary companies which now involved chemicals, timber and plywood. As a result, both Harrisons and Hudsons were effectively run as one, the Harrison subsidiary companies being either wound up or sold during 1978-80.

Both ships were crewed by British officers and Spanish ratings supplied by Harrisons although Hudson officers were occasionally seconded to serve from time to time. At the same time, on behalf of the same owner, the company undertook the technical management of two coastal gas tankers, **Gazala** (458grt/64) and **Karama** (500grt/65), and a landing barge, **Baraha** (263grt/76), all three ships operating in the Persian Gulf. The gas tankers were employed in transporting heating and cooking gas from Bahrain to Dubai while **Baraha** was used to transport road tankers loaded with water to oil refinery workers on an island in the Gulf. When the gas trade ceased in 1984, **Gazala** was broken up and **Karama** converted to a bunker tanker, **Baraha** having been already converted likewise in 1980 although the 1982/83 edition of *Lloyd's Register* still records her as a "landing barge".

Jumairah was delivered in November 1976 and her first voyage was a time charter to Hatim Shipping, Dubai, loading in Europe for Arabian Gulf ports. Following discharge, she ballasted to Malaysia to load plywood for Europe. **Mishref** was handed over in May 1977 and was chartered to Shaw Savill & Albion for a voyage from Avonmouth to Western Samoa, Fuji and New Zealand. She was then chartered to Mainland Chinese interests to load in Australia and New Zealand. In July 1977 she was chartered by the Swiss company Agratrade for a voyage to the east coast of South America and then to West Africa at a rate of $3,200 per day. After discharging at Port Harcourt, she ballasted to East London to load a cargo of grain for the Mersey for "FINEGRAIN" Cie Commerciale Agricole S A, Geneva, with the daily rate fixed at $3,000 per day.

Both the general cargo vessels were traded satisfactorily until the summer of 1978 when both were time chartered to an American company, Cargo Dispatching, owned by a Pakistani national which later turned out to be a fraudulent operation. **Jumairah** was first to go on hire and completed her period on hire before her sister. As a result of unpaid charter fees the company withdrew **Mishref** from the time charterer, even though she was in the middle of the charter and carrying cargo. **Jumairah** was proceeding to India and Pakistan to discharge. Informed that her discharge ports of Bombay and Karachi both had delays of sixty days, the ship was ordered to Dubai where she part discharged her cargo, completing discharge at Basrah in September. After discharge, she was detained for several days in respect of port charges and after release proceeded to Singapore for drydocking at Keppel Shipyard.

On completion of drydocking, *Jumairah* was chartered to Furness Withy and ballasted to Thevenard, South Australia, where she was sub-chartered to the Australian Barley Board to load barley for Basrah. She arrived at the Shat-al-Arab in the first week of December and did not berth at Basrah until the last week of March 1979. It was at this time that the two vessels were sold to a Greek owner and *Jumairah* sailed for Bahrain where she was laid up pending handing over to her new owners in May 1979, *Mishref* being laid up at Singapore at this time. *Mishref* discharged her last cargo in India and although Hudson had secured an excellent charter for her she proceeded to Singapore to lay up pending sale. Following her sale, *Mishref*'s first cargo was for a Danish timber exporter, loading in Malaya for UK/Continent. This company had been a regular customer while the ship was under Dubai ownership and *Jumairah* had performed the same charter to return to Europe after her maiden voyage to the Arabian Gulf. Relations between the Williams Hudson Group and the Ruler of Dubai had by now deteriorated to such a low level because of the financial losses incurred that the sale of the ships was handled by Common Brothers Ltd, Newcastle. At the same time, the Ruler of Dubai took over the total management of the two gas carriers and the landing barge.

During the late 1970s, the ultimate Group holding company was registered abroad. It was first registered in Panama as W H America S A, because David Rowland was based in New York and later in Luxembourg as W H Industries S A, when he became based in Europe.

THORNHOPE SHIPPING CO LTD : 1977 to 1988

Hudson Steamship was now manager for two ships, *Castle Point* and *Varangfjell*, which remained on charter to Olsen & Ugelstad until 1976 when the latter went bankrupt and Hudson Steamship now fixed cargoes and charters for her on the spot market. With John Hudson Fuel & Shipping Ltd. experiencing difficulty with its tanker operations the future looked bleak.

During 1973, Hudson Steamship had undertaken a study into the possibility of building larger colliers for service to the Thames using the then existing discharging gear. With the conclusions of the study Hudson Steamship convinced the CEGB that it was possible to operate a 12,500 dwt vessel supplying Thames power stations. The CEGB agreed to a ten year time charter with John Hudson Fuel & Shipping Ltd which negotiated a building contract in November 1973 with Robb Caledon Shipbuilders Ltd, Leith.

The building contract with Robb Caledon was subject to the approval of the Williams Hudson main board. The group was now experiencing very severe cash flow problems and Hudson Steamship was given fourteen days to find another owner for the newbuilding contract. In view of the sale of *Hudson Friendship* and *Hudson Venture* to Hilmar Reksten, Hudsons approached the Norwegians with the offer of the building contract with a secure long term charter. Reksten agreed to this, registering the newbuilding in the name of their English subsidiary, Thornhope Shipping Co Ltd.

The Thornhope Shipping Co Ltd had been established on 25 October 1924 to own the tramp steamer *Thornhope* (2272grt/24) and was owned by a Newcastle company, Alexanders Bros (T I & G Alexander Ltd). *Thornhope* was traded in the near trades to the Continent, Baltic and into the Mediterranean. Sold in 1937, she was renamed *Knitsley* and was torpedoed on 12 December 1942 off Lowestoft by German E-boat *S117*. In 1943, the Thornhope Shipping Co Ltd was sold to Hilmar Reksten. In 1970, orders were placed with Swan Hunter's Haverton Hill shipyard on the River Tees for two 169,000 dwt bulk carriers. Prior to this, Thornhope was a dormant company existing only on paper. With the company having no experience in the operation of large bulk carriers, Hilmar Reksten approached Furness Withy which had ordered a sister ship, *Furness Bridge*. As a result, the management of the two Thornhope ships, *Sir John Hunter* and *Sir Alexander Glen* was placed with the Furness Withy subsidiary Houlder Bros Ltd and the two ships operated in the Seabridge OBO pool.

Garrison Point. was launched on 5 August 1976. She was nine months late because Robb Caledon was involved in the construction of oil rigs at its Dundee yard and cited lack of technical personnel at Leith for the delays in construction of the vessel. Upon completion in January 1977, she began trading in the east coast coal trade on long term charter to the CEGB.

She is seen here, however, on the west coast of England, discharging coal at Bidston Dock, Birkenhead, on 24 May 1986.

(Roy Cressey)

*In 1979, **Varangfjell** was sold to her Mexican charterers Transportacion Maritima Mexicana SA. She had been on a two year time charter to them mainly carrying salt from the west coast of Mexico to Japan. At the end of the charter they had an option to purchase which they exercised. Within a matter of a week, they had immediately resold her for $12 million profit for further trading. Due to the speed of the sales, she had to be dry-docked three times in four weeks for classification requirements. With the sale of **Varangfjell**, the company was left with the management of only **Garrison Point**.*

(Donald MacFie, Dag Bakka jr collection)

In early 1979, Mr P K Arbuthnot was instructed by Williams Hudson to find a buyer for Hudson Steamship. Williams Hudson's financial situation had worsened due to poor investments in a Texas methanol refinery and a Canadian gold mine. The latter had been purchased in a redundant condition when the price of gold was very high. By the time it was in working condition, the price of gold had plummeted. Within a few years the group sold the shares in Vancouver Wharves which resulted in a £4 million deficit, coupled to extraordinary charges of £12 million related to the disposal of American subsidiaries. Aware of the position, Thornhope Shipping Co Ltd had first offered to buy Hudson Steamship in October 1978 and by the time David Rowland agreed he would sell Hudson Steamship to Thornhope Shipping Co Ltd, the Ruler of Dubai had decided to sell his two Santa Fe type general cargo ships. With the loss of the management of the five Dubai ships, Hudson Steamship would only have two ships to manage and Thornhope held back from buying Hudson Steamship for the moment. At that time they had only been prepared to transfer the management of the bulk carrier **Sir Alexander Glen** in exchange for ownership of Hudson Steamship.

Thornhope's Superintendent, Mr H Orvik, had been involved with the setting up of the Arab Maritime Petroleum Company. His experience with this organisation had underlined the problems in setting up a ship management company and Thornhope was interested in acquiring a going concern. At the time, Hudson Steamship owned a 25% shareholding in Ships Electronic Services Ltd whose business was mainly supply and repair of ship's radio equipment and this shareholding was sold prior to the takeover. Through the intervention again of Per Mender, Hudson Steamship was sold to the Norwegian shipowner Lars Krogh.

Hudson Steamship was recapitalised in 1980 with an issue of shares worth £50,000 and sold by the Williams Hudson Group Ltd. Hudson Steamship became a wholly owned subsidiary of Oslo-based Lars Krogh A/S. At the same time that they acquired Hudson Steamship, Lars Krogh also bought an "off-the-shelf" company, Sanhob Ltd. The assets of this company were switched with Hudson Steamship so Lars Krogh would not be liable for any debts owed by Hudson Steamship while it was owned by the Williams Hudson Group. On 18 March 1980, Sanhob Ltd's directors approved the decision to change its trading name to Hudson Steamship Co Ltd. Shortly after the takeover, Hudson Steamship returned to Brighton, setting up offices at 25, Ship Street. On 31 March 1980, Mr P K Arbuthnot and Mr C Holmes resigned as Managing Director and Company Secretary of the "old" Hudson Steamship and were appointed to the "new" company, formerly Sanhob Ltd. They also resigned from the board of John Hudson Fuel & Shipping Ltd where they were Director and Company Secretary respectively. At the time of the sale there were only two other directors on the "old" company's board, Mr David Rowland and Mr J E James. As a result of the takeover, Lars Krogh and his great friend Per Mender joined Hudson Steamship's board as directors on 6 May 1980.

On 1 March 1983, the Williams Hudson Group was wound up. John Hudson & Co Ltd was sold for £600,000 in 1981 to the German company RAAB Karcher. They would appear to have purchased a dormant Williams Hudson Group company, Brainwaith Ltd, and switched the assets of John Hudson & Co Ltd in a move similar to Lars Krogh when he purchased Hudson Steamship. As of 5 November 1981, Brainwaith Ltd traded as John Hudson & Co Ltd, changing its name to John Hudson & Company in 1982 although it has been dormant since December 1991. In the late 1970s, the Carless Capel Group, formerly Carless, Capel & Leonard, had negotiated to buy John Hudson & Co Ltd from the Williams Hudson Group but had been unsuccessful. John Hudson Fuel & Shipping Ltd changed its name on 5 November 1981 to Brainwaith Shipping Ltd. Its business was described as shipowners and managers although the company never actually owned or managed vessels. From July 1982 it became a dormant company and was wound up in July 1987.

Following the purchase of Hudson Steamship by Lars Krogh, Thornhope Shipping Co Ltd bought two bulk carriers from foreign owners which were placed under Hudson Steamship management. Both ships were fixed with short term charters to the CEGB. Because of Hudson Steamship's instability at the time, CEGB considered terminating **Garrison Point**'s charter unless the company showed that they managed a further two British-flagged vessels. During negotiations between Thornhope and Hudson Steamship, the possibility of a long term agreement between Hudson Steamship and John Hudson Fuel & Shipping Ltd was considered. This would have meant an easy return to shipowning for the Williams Hudson Group. However this was not to be.

It was ironic that after diversifying away from the collier trade in the 1950s and 1960s the company should return to it, albeit as managers, with three ships in the 1980s. The first ship to be delivered was the two year old **Warden Point** which had been built for a Swedish consortium as **Red Sea** and she was handed over in October. One of five similar vessels, she was a gearless, two-hatch ship of 6,900 dwt. Built with an icebreaker bow, she was flush-decked from her foc'sle aft, and had a five tier deck house placed on her stern which gave her a distinctive profile. Her two box-shaped holds allowed her to carry containers as she had been designed for general trading.

The **Warden Point** arrives at Leith on 20 July 1986.

(Ian Willett)

She was joined in December 1980 by **Crusader Point** which had recently been built in East Germany for German-based Singapore owners. A two-hatch, geared general cargo ship, she was one of a standard class designed by her builders. After she was acquired, she drydocked at South Shields where her cargo derricks were removed so that her cargo capacity was increased. After she had been in service for a couple of years, her main mast was removed to further increase her deadweight which left her with a goalpost mast built into the accommodation front and a foremast on the focsle. When the Hadley Steamship Co Ltd purchased a sistership, **Clymene**, which was also chartered to the CEGB, she had her derricks removed, but after her charter ended they were refitted prior to returning to general trading. The finance for the purchase of **Warden Point** was provided by Investors in Industry PLC, later 3i plc, while the company approached Hambros Bank for the finance for **Crusader Point**. Hudson Steamship was able to negotiate a five year charter for **Warden Point** to the Central Electricity Generating Board with a further five year option.

On entry into service, the **Crusader Point** obtained an initial six year charter to the Central Electricity Generating Board with a four year extension option.

(World Ship Photo Library)

The **Carsol** laid up in London's Regent Dock on 27 December 1980. Of 1,067dwt, she was fitted with eight cargo tanks.

(Author's collection)

The company also returned to the tanker trades in 1979 when it was approached by Carless Solvents Ltd, a member of the Carless Capel Group, to find a suitable coastal tanker on its behalf. One of Carless Solvents' directors, Mr A K Reynolds, had been the Managing Director of Hudson Steamship until 1972 and also a main board member of the Williams Group who was aware of the company's management experience. As a result, Carless Solvents purchased a fifteen year old Danish tanker, **Lisbet Terkol** (500grt/64), which had been laid up at Fredericia since August 1979 and renamed her **Carsol** under Hudson Steamship management. A charter was arranged with the CEGB for the transfer of oil between various power stations. However, on her delivery voyage from Århus to the Thames she suffered serious engine failure and had to be repaired in Bremen. After this initial setback, she commenced working for the CEGB and after that charter expired she was employed on a series of short time charters principally to Rowbotham Tankships Ltd and single voyage fixings.

As a result of discussions between Carless Solvents, Hudson Steamship and the CEGB, Hudson Steamship obtained quotations for the construction of a 7,700dwt bulk carrier suitable for long term charter to the CEGB. Carless Solvents Ltd would be the registered owners with Hudson Steamship as managers. The contract for the vessel was signed on 26 April 1980 with the Japanese company Mitsubishi which subcontracted the order to the Miho Shipyard. Launched on 7 October 1981 as **Landguard Point**, she ran trials off Shimizu on 12 and 14 December 1981.

A single-screw vessel, she was powered by an Akasaka-Mitsubishi diesel and had a bow thruster. Her service speed was 13 knots with a fuel consumption of 16.5 tons per day and she was a gearless three hatch/three hold vessel, although provision was made by her builders for a gantry type twin crane to be installed over No 2 hatch at a later date. The hatch coaming was reinforced for this crane which was never fitted and she also had a 188 TEU container capacity. Accommodation was provided for 23 crew plus a pilot, in single cabins. Handed over by her builders on 4 January 1982, the **Landguard Point** sailed in ballast for Guyana to load sugar for London. After discharge, she went on charter to the CEGB. She was named after Landguard Point in Suffolk, near the main Carless chemical plant in the UK. Her maiden voyage was under the command of Captain Horsley and is notable because the ship carried the company's one and only female Second Officer who could have been the first female collier Master had she not emigrated to Australia. From 1976 until 1982, the company employed a number of female Radio Officers.

In 1981, Thornhope Shipping Co Ltd purchased 37,502 shares in Hudson Steamship from Lars Krogh giving the company a 75% stake in Hudson Steamship. Per Mender resigned as a director and two new directors, H Ovrevik and R Barlow, Thornhope's Managing Director and Company Secretary, joined Hudson Steamship as non-executive directors. The following year Thornhope purchased the remaining 25% of Hudson Steamship's shareholding, 12,499 shares, from Lars Krogh, who left the board of Hudson Steamship on 30 November 1982.

Following the resignation of Hector Ovrevik from both Thornhope Shipping Co Ltd and Hudson Steamship in June 1982, Mr Arbuthnot was appointed to the board of Thornhope Shipping Co Ltd as of 1 July 1982. Mr Holmes was also appointed to the board of Thornhope Shipping Co Ltd in January 1983. Mr Barlow left the boards of both companies in July 1983, his place on the board of Hudson Steamship being taken by Mr A P Follett who had joined the company in 1968 as Operations Manager when the company took over the day-to-day running of its own ships.

In 1983, Thornhope Shipping Co Ltd switched management of its 169,000 dwt OBO (oil/bulk/ore) **Sir Alexander Glen**, from Denholm Ship Management Ltd to Hudson Steamship. After her management was transferred, she operated worldwide in the Seateam OBO pool until 1986. During her time in the pool, her cargoes ranged from oil loaded in the Arabian Gulf or Libya to bulk coal and iron ore from Australia, Africa or the USA. Launched in November 1974 and handed over in April 1975, she had a deadweight of 169,080 tonnes on a draught of 18,442 metres. Accommodation was provided for forty-three crew with three cadets. She had a voyage range of 26,000 miles at a service speed of 15.75 knots. Her fuel consumption was officially 108 tons of heavy fuel per day.

While transferring **Sir Alexander Glen** to Hudson Steamship, it is interesting to note that when Thornhope purchased **Sir Charles Hambro** in March 1986 she remained under the Norwegian flag with Reksten, her former owners, as managers. Her sale to Iranian owners in 1988 raised $14.5 million. Having only paid $5.5 million to Reksten for the vessel, Thornhope Shipping Co Ltd was liable for a large tax bill which did nothing for its financial position. In an attempt to raise capital in 1983, Thornhope Shipping Co Ltd had sold the 17.5% shareholding which it held in the Kingsnorth Marine Drilling Co Ltd.

The company now managed a fleet of six vessels. Four were on charter to CEGB with **Sir Alexander Glen** employed worldwide although **Carsol** was sold to Greek owners in August 1982 after having been laid up in the London's Royal Docks since January 1981 when it had become difficult to find work for her. A new holding company, Thornhope Ltd, was set up in 1984 for Thornhope Shipping Co Ltd and Hudson Steamship. By now, Thornhope Shipping Co Ltd was a subsidiary of Palmeston Holdings which was itself a subsidiary of a Liberian company, Cornhill Shipping Ltd. Both **Sir Alexander Glen** and **Garrison Point** were now transferred to the ownership of Thornhope Ltd.

In early 1984, the National Union of Mineworkers called a strike over proposed colliery closures. With no coal being mined in the United Kingdom and the refusal of the Thames power station workers to discharge foreign imports, the company's ships were laid up. Large coal stocks at the power stations coupled with a warm summer and mild winter meant the strike lasted for almost twelve months before coal production resumed. While the remaining four CEGB owned ships were employed away from the coast, mainly in the scrap trade to Spain, the company's ships were laid up. **Garrison Point** and **Crusader Point** were both laid up at Blyth. The latter only made one voyage from lay up, sailing from Blyth to Shannon to load a return cargo of alumina for Blyth. **Landguard Point** fared a little better. Laid up at Hartlepool, she secured several cargoes from France to the Thames allowing the company's Masters to retain their Thames pilotage exemption. After initially being laid up at Ipswich, **Warden Point** was drydocked on the Tyne and then laid up at Jarrow. All ships were kept fully crewed waiting for the strike to end. Because of the strike and the lack of opportunity of cargoes for their ships, the company made an operating loss of £1,688 in 1984.

The coal miners' strike ended in April 1985 and the ships returned to trade although **Crusader Point** and **Landguard Point** were laid up on several occasions as demand for coal dropped and they were not needed. With the possibility of losing CEGB charters, it was felt the company should not rely solely on CEGB work and a six year old mini bulk carrier, **Coral** (1599grt/79), was purchased from Spanish owners in July 1985. Initially she was registered under the ownership of a Liberian company, Senior Navigation Co Ltd, flying the Bahamas flag, but was later transferred to the ownership of Thornhope Shipping Co Ltd while still continuing under Bahamian registration. She was operated in the Bulkship (Nederland) BV pool, a consortium of European coaster operators, and traded in northern Europe, the Baltic, and as far south as Casablanca.

For the first time the company manned a ship with a foreign crew, employing Polish ratings. During the early 1980s, the company had negotiated new working practices with the National Union of Seamen so that the company was not tied to the North East Coast Agreement which governed pay and conditions for crews chartered to CEGB. The crews were now paid a fixed weekly rate taking into account overtime and weekend work. As a result of an incident in Taiwan in 1985 when **Sir Alexander Glen** suffered a fire in her accommodation started deliberately by one of her ratings, the company decided to crew her with British officers and Chinese ratings. At the same time she was switched to the Hong Kong register and in 1987 Polish crew replaced the Chinese ratings.

On 21 February 1986, Carless Solvents informed Hudson Steamship they intended to sell **Landguard Point** and withdraw from shipowning. In June 1986, both **Landguard Point** and **Crusader Point** went off charter from the CEGB and were laid up at Hartlepool. At the same time **Castle Point**, ex **Hudson Light**, was also laid up at Hartlepool along with the three remaining 1960s colliers owned by the CEGB, all six ships being displaced by the introduction of three larger colliers by the CEGB, managed by Christian Salvesen Ltd. When the four CEGB colliers were sold to Panamanian flag operators, **Castle Point** was renamed **Sonia 1**, the first three letters of her new name being still welded on her hull from her service as **Hudson Light**. She was drydocked at Middlesbrough prior to handing over and was the first ship to be drydocked at the former Smiths Docks which had been closed for five years when she arrived on 16 January 1988. At this time, **Sir Alexander Glen** was withdrawn from the Seateam pool and traded on the spot market. While operating in the Seateam pool she only once visited the UK in 1983 when she discharged part of a cargo of iron ore at Port Talbot. This left only **Garrison Point** and **Warden Point** with guaranteed work.

*In 1981, **Garrison Point** was sent to load coal in New Orleans for the CEGB. Sailing from Tilbury on 10 January she crossed the Atlantic arriving at New Orleans on 28 January. She sailed the next day for the Thames and arrived there on 17 February, making this the longest voyage for a direct coal shipment to the Thames power stations and it was at a Thames power station that she was photographed on 16 January 1977.*

(Company archives)

In September 1986, **Landguard Point** was sold to Bahamian owners and handed over on 21 October at North Shields after a pre-sale drydocking. Renamed **Mrs B**, she was later resold to Yugoslavian owners and in 1991 resold to Australian owners for conversion to a hot cargo chemical tanker for a dedicated service between Australia and China. At the end of 1986, **Crusader Point** was sold to German owners after her leasing agreement was ended by Thornhope Shipping Co Ltd on 22 December. In January 1987, she sailed from lay up to Sunderland for minor structural steelwork before sailing to Hamburg where she was lengthened and converted to a chemical tanker. Since her sale she has undergone several changes of name and owners and currently trades in European waters under the Norwegian flag. In January 1987, **Garrison Point** came off charter to the CEGB and was returned to the company. An initial result of this move was that she was repainted in Hudson colours having previously borne CEGB funnel markings. The company was able to find work for her throughout 1987 in northern Europe while **Warden Point** continued on a short term charter to CEGB.

Hudson Steamship now found itself in a difficult position as a result of debts incurred from Thornhope Shipping Co Ltd. While Hudson Steamship had continued to manage ships on behalf of Thornhope Co Ltd, both existed as separate companies and Hudson Steamship continued to make an operating loss throughout the late 1980s. Although Hudson Steamship had made a profit of £190,331 in 1986, £226,912 was owed by group companies which was assumed to be recoverable. In 1987 Hudson Steamship's accounts showed Thornhope Ltd owed £258,960 in management fees which were not expected to be paid. Hudson Steamship was then instructed by Thornhope Ltd to find a buyer for both themselves and Thornhope Shipping Co Ltd. **Sir Alexander Glen** and **Garrison Point** were transferred back to the ownership of the Thornhope Shipping Co Ltd and again Per Mender was involved in negotiating the sale of the two companies. In December 1987, Thornhope Ltd, which was liquidated in 1992, sold both Thornhope Shipping Co Ltd and Hudson Steamship to Mosvold Shipping A/S, Kristiansand.

Warden Point

(Company archives)

MOSVOLD SHIPPING A/S : 1988 to 1996

Mosvold Shipping was an established company with experience in operating large bulk carriers and tankers although in 1988 they only owned one vessel, **Mosbulk** (74003grt/85). At the time of the takeover, Mosvold announced that Hudson Steamship would be used as the ship management company for the Mosvold group although they would retain management of **Mosbulk**. Shortly after the takeover, **Mosbulk** was sold to her time charterers, P & O Bulk Shipping, which had an option to purchase the vessel and the Mosvold ship management team was disbanded. Just prior to the take over of Thornhope Shipping Co Ltd and Hudson Steamship, Mosvold acquired the shareholding of a Danish ship investment company, D/S A/S Progress, publicly quoted at DKK 52.2 million giving Mosvold a part ownership in two OBO newbuildings.

Both **Garrison Point** and **Sir Alexander Glen** were transferred to the Bahamian register. At the time of the takeover **Garrison Point** was undergoing a drydocking at North Shields. She was renamed **Elizabete** and her funnel repainted in Mosvold colours, a five ring Olympian device. Her new name revived one of the war-managed Estonian ships. Originally Polish seafarers were employed on her but after protests from the unions British crew were employed. **Coral** and **Warden Point** remained unaffected by the takeover as far as trade patterns and crewing were concerned.

Prior to the takeover, both Thornhope Shipping Co Ltd and Hudson Steamship had only three directors on their respective boards. Mr J M Clay, who had been on the board of Thornhope Shipping Co Ltd since 1970, resigned shortly after the takeover. He was Deputy Chairman of Hambros Bank and a Director of the Bank of England until he resigned from that post in 1987 because of Hambros' involvement in disputes over Hilmar Reksten's finances. In his place Mosvolds appointed two new directors from their company, K F Mosvold and M Borge. Later the Managing Director of Uddevalla Shipping, G Rosengren, was appointed Chairman and Director of the Thornhope Shipping Co Ltd although he was only a board member until December 1988.

Since 1983, the board of Hudson Steamship had comprised Mr Arbuthnot and two other directors, Mr A P Follett and Mr K Vipan, Mr C.Holmes continuing as Company Secretary. Both were long serving company personnel: Mr Vipan had joined the company in 1972 as Engineer Superintendent, Mr Follett joining the company in 1968 as Operations Manager. Mr Follett actually retired on 31 December 1987, his 65th birthday, the day before Mosvold took over Hudson Steamship and Thornhope Shipping Co Ltd. No additions were made to the board until January 1989 when Mosvold's Chief Accountant, Mr M Kristiansen, became a director and Mr E Ribe, its Chief Superintendent, became Chairman and Director. Also appointed to the board was Captain F Davies who had joined the company in 1972. He served on the VLCCs as a Second Officer and in 1978 was sent to Dubai to work in the office of the Harrison's office cleaning subsidiary. Made redundant in 1979, he was re-employed by Hudson Steamship in 1981 and served on all the company's vessels. In 1988 he came into the office to understudy Mr Follet whom he succeeded as Operations Manager in 1988.

In 1988 the Norwegian Government implemented a scheme whereby it was beneficial for individuals through tax benefits to invest in shipping and as a result KS, or limited companies, were set up. By attracting their investors, Mosvolds were able to set up a number of KS companies. One of the rules governing the KS companies was that a major part of the company's operation had to take place in Norway, similar to the agreement which saw the company operate **Bel-Hudson**, and that vessels should fly the Norwegian flag. Mosvold had overall control of the vessels while commercial management of the ships was undertaken by a subsidiary Mosvold company NOR-OBO Shipping, Grimstad, to whom the ships were chartered,and then sub-chartered or fixed on the spot market. NOR-OBO Shipping was set up in April 1988 and had a total capital of NOK 23 million. Personnel and technical management of the vessels was handed over to Hudson Steamship. Mosvold's stated policy at the time of the takeover of Hudson Steamship was to buy and sell vessels as and when the opportunity arose. Vessels owned by KS companies generally bore the funnel markings of NOR-OBO unless a charterer requested its own funnel markings.

The first vessel to be transferred to Hudson management was delivered in August 1988. Purchased from Cypriot owners, she was renamed **Mosstar** and registered under the ownership of the Thornhope Shipping Co Ltd with the funnel markings of Hudson Steamship and was placed on the Norwegian International Ship (NIS) Register. A general cargo tweendecker of 16,000 dwt, she traded on the spot market. By the end of 1988, Mosvolds acquired a further four ships. September saw the purchase of a general cargo ship, which was renamed **Mostween 2**, and was followed in December by a tanker from Greek owners which was renamed **Mostank**. Another general cargo ship, renamed **Mosbay**, was also purchased in December and taken over in Japan. During her time in the fleet, she was fixed on several charters to the Danish companies Lauritzen and Dannebrog. All three ships were registered under the ownership of separate KS companies and placed on the NIS Register.

The **Mostween 2** with a full cargo of timber.

(Author's collection)

The final ship to be purchased in 1988 was a container vessel, **Ostfriesland**, from German-backed Cypriot owners which was secured by a long-term time charter to Lloyd Brasileiro. **Ostfriesland** was not renamed although she too was registered under a KS company and placed on the Norwegian International Ship Register.

(Author's collection)

1989 began with the sale of **Sir Alexander Glen** to Taiwanese owners. Handed over in Rotterdam, she was renamed **Sir Alexander** under the Cypriot flag. She never traded under this name and was later renamed **Ocean Mandarin** and transferred to Taiwan registry. Her new owners also operated a sistership, **Ocean Sovereign**, under the Cypriot flag built as **Furness Bridge** and broken up in 1992. **Ocean Mandarin** was reported as being sold to Chinese breakers in 1993, her poor structural condition attracting interest as she was a sister of the ill-fated **Derbyshire** which was lost in 1980 in the Pacific and whose wreckage was found in mid-1994. However the report of her demolition proved in error. In 1994 she was arrested in South Korea after losing her rudder on passage from Canada to South Korea with a cargo of coal. While under arrest she underwent a port state control inspection which she failed on nineteen counts. She never traded again and was sold for demolition sailing from South Korea during November 1994 for Xinhui to be broken up. The last of these sisters from the class of six ships was the second Thornhope ship, **Sir John Hunter**, which was scrapped in 1997 as **Nafsika M**. As a result of the concern raised by the loss of **Derbyshire** in April 1982, **Sir Alexander Glen**, when still under Denholm management, was inspected by her officers and found to have fractures in the area around Frame 65. Temporary repairs were effected at Taranto although two months later a follow-up survey found new fractures on her starboard side resulting in further repairs in Osaka. While under Hudson Steamship management, she was regularly inspected by her crew for further fractures.

In February, **Mostween 4** was purchased from Cypriot owners and went on charter to Longo Shipping until May 1990, while in April **Mostween 5** joined the fleet from Greek owners for $5.725 million having being superficially inspected at Genoa in January. Upon purchase she went on charter to the Danish company Freja until March 1990. June saw a further three ships purchased, the general cargo ship **Mostween 6** from Cypriot operators, **Mostween 8** from Greek owners and the geared bulk carrier **Mosdeep** from Bahamian owners associated with the East Asiatic Company, Copenhagen. The first four ships were registered under the NIS Register and **Mosdeep** was placed under the ownership of Thornhope Shipping Co Ltd, flying the Bahamas flag. Hudson Steamship secured a nine-year time charter for her from June 1989 to Fednav of Canada on a dedicated service shipping nickel ore from Indonesia to Townsville. At the end of her charter in June 1998 the charter party clause provided for the sale of the vessel on the open market, Fednav receiving 50% of the net sale price as a discount on hire paid under the charter party. The only other ship of this group to obtain charter work was **Mostween 8**, which was chartered to Lloyd Brasiliero initially for twelve months from August 1990 trading between South America and the Far East. The other ships traded on the spot market.

Further additions were made in July when **Mostween 7** and **Mos Freeway** were acquired. **Mos Freeway** was a roll-on/roll-off vessel bought for a five year charter to P & O. Built in 1982, she had a capacity for 101 trailers, 284 TEU on wheeled flats and 158 cars. Two full length mobile car decks installed immediately above the main deck allowed this configuration to be altered to 60 trailers, 120 TEU and 537 cars. Placed under Thornhope Shipping Co Ltd ownership, she was laid up at Gibraltar as the charter fell through shortly after her purchase. She was later sold to Spanish owners in January 1990 for $9,650,000. The second half of 1990 saw three geared bulk carriers purchased, **Mosgulf**, **Mosriver** and **Moslake**. All three ships were built in the 1970s and were registered in the ownership of KS companies. **Mosgulf** was taken over on 16 August 1989 at Ghent, being placed on charter to Galleon Shipping, part of the Danish Freya group. They in turn subchartered her on several occasions to other companies.

Mostween 7 was placed under the ownership of a KS company following purchase. She was photographed as she passed Gravesend on 2 April 1995. *(Ian Willett)*

After less than a year, **Mostween 2** was disposed of to Jordanian owners in August 1989. **Mostank** was sold for $19.15 million to Norwegian owners and was handed over at Abidjan, Ivory Coast, on 26 September 1989. She had traded world-wide on the spot market although for the last five months she had been trading principally in the South Atlantic.

Elizabete was sold to Stephenson Clarke Shipping Ltd for £2,512,000 in September 1989 and handed over at Sunderland. Since finishing her CEGB charter, she had traded on the spot market although a great deal of her cargoes had been for Stephenson Clarke and it was no surprise that they purchased her. Following her sale she was renamed **Jevington** and remained registered in the Bahamas.

While the first eighteen months of Mosvold ownership had seen a rise in the number of ships managed, 1990 saw a slow down of acquisitions. **Ostfriesland** was bought by Singapore owners for $10,875,000 with a charter back for three years to NOR-OBO. The only new business gained in 1990 was a twelve month contract for the technical management of a Cypriot-registered container ship, **Patricia**. Hudson Steamship were approached by Isle of Man-based Mid Ocean Maritime Ltd which had been appointed managers of the vessel by her owners, Peter Dohle GmbH, Hamburg. A subsidiary company, Mid Ocean Technical Services Ltd, was formed with the specific task of technical management of **Patricia**. At the end of the contract in 1991, Mid Ocean Technical Services Ltd ceased to be an active company.

During 1989, Hudson Steamship formed a venture company, HMS Shipping Co Ltd, based in the Philippines. It was a 50/50 venture with Philippines shipowner Carlos Salinas who also controlled one of the crew agencies used by Hudson Steamship. However this company never actively traded and was wound up in 1994.

In February 1990, **Warden Point** was sold to Australian owners for service as a self-discharging cement carrier on the Australian coast. Having come off charter to CEGB on 11 December 1989, she was fixed for a cargo from Dublin to Crotone near Taranto in Italy. She remained in the Mediterranean until February 1990 when she returned to Rotterdam. She then proceeded to Hamburg to load the cargo handling gear required for her conversion, which was designed by Kvaerner. Sailing on 3 March from Hamburg, she called at Istanbul and Jeddah before arriving at Singapore where the cargo gear was fitted. She continued on to Australia, arriving at Cairns on 22 May and was handed over to her new owners the following day. She was sold without a change of name and Hudson Steamship retained management of the vessel for the delivery voyage from Europe to Australia. On the outward passage she was transferred to the Bahamas register and was re-registered as an Australian-flagged vessel prior to her entering her new trade.

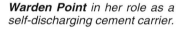

Warden Point in her role as a self-discharging cement carrier.

(Russell Priest)

1990 was a bad year financially for Hudson Steamship. It made a loss after tax of £130,675, which the company blamed on redundancy payments and the poor exchange rate of the US dollar. This was in contrast to 1989 when the company made a profit of £71,583 on a turnover of £514,622. In the first year of ownership by Mosvold it only had a turnover of £198,574 with a loss of £8,536, after tax. In Group terms Mosvold's gross operating income from shipping fell from NOK 156 million in 1989 to NOK 114 million in 1990. This was due to a reduction in the fleet because of sales and reduced income from the remaining owned vessels. The sale of vessels at this time realised a total of $51 million of which Mosvold's share through their part owning of the K/S companies was $25 million.

In 1991, **Mosstar** was chartered to the United States Sealift Command for service during the Gulf War. This was her second such charter and she went on charter at Wilmington on 5 February 1991 loading 9,000 tons of explosives. On 28 February she arrived off Falmouth and remained at anchor, still on hire, until 8 November 1991 when she sailed for San Francisco. In October she had been sold for $4.67 million to Dalarik Shipping Co, Cyprus, which bareboat chartered her to NOR-OBO until her redelivery at San Francisco, where she arrived on 15 December 1991. She was subsequently handed over to Dalarik on 23 December.

Mostween 6

(Company archives)

In August 1991, **Mosbay** was sold for $8.05 million to Turkish owners and handed over on 24 August after dry-docking at Singapore. **Mostween 6**, which for a short time in 1991 at the request of her charterers had been renamed **Hyacinth Trader**, was sold in October 1991 for $4.55 million to Hong Kong based owners and **Mostween 4** left the fleet in December passing to Greek owners for $4.35 million.

Two Panamax type bulk carriers were purchased from South Korean shipbuilders in October 1991 having originally been ordered by the Czechoslovakian state shipping company Czechoslovak Ocean Shipping International Joint Stock Co, Prague, and laid up after the Czechs had refused delivery. Completed for Mosvold as **Mosdale** and **Moshill**, they had been laid down in July and December 1989 with **Moshill**'s keel being laid three days after the launch of **Mosdale** on 16 December. **Moshill** was launched on 28 April 1990. Both ships were then laid up at the builder's yard in the hope that a buyer would come forward. As it was, Mosvold signed contracts for the completion of both vessels on 23 September 1991 and they were named in a joint ceremony on 7 October 1991. Both ships were registered under the ownership of Mosvold Shipping A/S and carried Mosvold colours as opposed to NOR-OBO. It was originally intended to trade these ships under the Norwegian International Ship Register but this was later changed and both ships went under the Bahamas Register. Both were employed loading coal in Australia for Japan and the eastern seaboard of Russia. The acquisition of these vessels was part of a strategic decision to consolidate the Group's shipping activities into the Danish-listed D/S A/S Progress. However this consolidation could not be completed and as a result the vessels were sold in December 1991 with delivery scheduled for February and March 1992. They were sold for $28.9 million each, having been purchased from the builders for a total price of $56.3 million. During 1991, Hudson Steamship was awarded the Bureau Veritas Quality Certificate of Approval for Ship Management & Operations to the BS5750 Standard Part 2, making them one of a small number of companies to attain this award. Hudson Steamship withdrew from the coastal trades with the sale of **Coral** which was handed over in Rotterdam on 3 December 1991 to a Dutch company within the Bulkship (Nederland) BV pool. Her sale raised $2.225 million but during that financial year Hudson Steamship made a loss after tax of £84,257.

Throughout 1992, the KS company owned ships continued to be sold due to a lack of investment in the KS schemes. **Mostween 8** was sold to Liberian owners for $2.85 million and had been on charter to Lloyd Brasileiro until September 1992. **Mosgulf** was handed over to St Vincent flag owners, which were ultimately controlled by the People's Republic of China, at Shekou on 3 September. Since April 1992, she had been on charter to Ocean Link trading mainly to Chinese ports. On 14 May she had collided with a Chinese inshore fishing vessel shortly after sailing from Qinhuangdao and was arrested and detained at Shidao for five days.

Through **Mosdeep**'s Fednav charter, Hudson Steamship took over the management of Fednav's roll-on/roll-off vessel **ASL Cygnus** on 1 April 1992. Originally built for the German company Hansa which went into liquidation in the early 1980s, the four ships in her class were notable as being the first Hansa ships for some time not to be fitted with heavy lift derricks. Sold to Lykes Bros, New Orleans, she had been chartered to the American Government until sold to Fednav in 1990. Under the Bahamas flag, shortly after her transfer to Hudson management, she was chartered to Wilh. Wilhelmsen for a service from South Africa to the United States and was renamed **Thekwini**, the Zulu name for the South African city of Durban. Fednav also took over another sister, named **ASL Sanderling** but she did not pass to Hudson Steamship management.

Outside management was also undertaken on behalf of the French company, Armement Marseilles Fret S A which transferred three ships from a Cypriot management company to Hudson Steamship. The first two ships to be transferred were roll-on/roll-off sisterships **Evening Star** and **Guyane**. Both were Cypriot flag vessels registered under the ownership of Armement Marseilles Fret subsidiaries Morena Shipping and Blue Shire Marine. Both ships had been built in Italy in 1979 and had been laid up following their launching after their owners, Traghetti del Mediterraneo, had gone bankrupt. Their builders sold them to Indonesian owners in 1981 and were bought by Armement Marseilles Fret

A rare view of the **Evening Star** and **Guyane** together on 19 March 1992.

(Author's collection)

during 1988 for a Europe-Caribbean service. The third ship was a general cargo ship originally built in Poland for Elder Dempster from whom she was purchased in 1987. Renamed **Antilles** under the French flag, she was later renamed **Saint Pierre** and transferred to Cypriot registry. Like the two other ships, she traded from the Mediterranean to the Caribbean and North and South America.

On 31 March 1992, Mr P K Arbuthnot retired as Managing Director of both Thornhope Shipping Co Ltd and Hudson Steamship. Captain Davies was appointed his successor as Managing Director of Hudson Steamship. Until the company's closure in 1996, there were two further additions to the board of Hudson Steamship. Mr M Penfold was appointed Technical Director in June 1992; he had previously served as Chief Engineer in the VLCCs and had been the company's Engineer Superintendent before being made redundant in 1980. He rejoined the company after the resignation of Mr Vipan. In February 1995, Mr J Kaspersen, Mosvold's Chartering and Operations Manager and manager of NOR-OBO, joined the board.

In April 1993, the sale of KS owned shipping continued when **Moslake** was sold to the People's Republic of China and like **Mosgulf** she was registered in St. Vincent & Grenadines. **Thekwini** was sold for $15.85 million to the United States Military Sealift Command. She was one of twelve roll-on roll-off and multi purpose vessels purchased from various owners for approximately £270 million for the American Ready Reserve fleet. Throughout 1993, the company continued to manage **Mostween 5**, **Mostween 7**, **Mosdeep** and **Mosriver**. In April 1993, management of the three Cypriot vessels was taken over by Armement Marseilles Fret S A which had decided to manage the three vessels itself.

While Norwegian masters were employed on the Mosvold vessels, crews for all ships were taken from the former Yugoslavia, Poland and the Philippines, where the company used two main crewing agencies. At the same time the company was actively looking for new ship management work and carrying out technical inspections of vessels for other owners and reporting on their vessels' condition. The company also carried out work on the production of manuals, policy documents and advice on quality assurance matters for an Isle of Man based company. At the same time, manuals and policy documents were produced for the company's own managed ships, being part of its own ISO and ISM systems.

Mostween 5 was renamed **Napier Star** for a time charter to Blue Star Line in July 1993, trading from the west coast of America and Canada across to the Pacific islands and New Zealand. Upon completion of this charter in August 1994 she reverted to **Mostween 5**.

In November 1993, Mosvold Shipping purchased a 1974-built VLCC from Esso International Shipping (Bahamas) Ltd. Built as **Esso Saba** she had been renamed **Esso Freeport** after transfer to the Bahamas register. Laid up for several years in the Far East and having undergone a major dry-docking prior to her sale, the vessel was in extremely good condition for her age, her lay up period helping to extend her life expectancy. Registered under the ownership of Thornhope Shipping Co Ltd, she was renamed **Moscliff** on the Bahamas Register. Shortly after her purchase, she underwent a CAP survey (Condition Assessment Programme) performed by Det Norske Veritas and was awarded a Level 4. These assessments are graded on a scale of 1 to 5 with 5 being awarded to newbuildings.

Bearing the funnel colours of the Thornhope Shipping Co Ltd, the **Crusader Point** was photographed as she was loading coal on the River Tyne on 2 June 1987.

(World Ship Photo Library)

Another view of the **Crusader Point**, but now with her funnel now displaying Hudson colours. She is passing Tilbury on her way down the River Thames.

(World Ship Photo Library)

With the quayside and buildings of North Shields in the background, the **Warden Point** is about to drop the Tyne pilot as she leaves the river with a full cargo of coal on 15 August 1981.

(World Ship Photo Library)

The **Warden Point**, now registered in Brisbane, looks very different in her role as a self-discharging cement carrier working for The Queensland Cement & Lime Company Limited.

(Russell Priest)

The Hudson company's venture into tanker operation was a bold move but had very mixed fortunes. The appropriately-named **Hudson Venture** was photographed on the New Waterway on 31 August 1971.

(World Ship Photo Library)

The Hudson funnel colours would be seen by everyone driving along the dock road in Liverpool but the laid-up STAT 32 tanker **Hudson Deep** was hardly a good advertisement for the company. The photograph was taken on 28 May 1978.

(World Ship Photo Library)

The four STAT 32 tankers eventually saw excellent service as fleet auxiliaries. The **Appleleaf** was photographed irom the frigate **HMS Penelope** in the dramatic setting of South Georgia shortly after the British forces had won control of the Falklands Islands in 1982.

(Paul Silsby, courtesy of Ron Baker)

Built as **Hudson Cavalier**, the **Appleleaf** was bought by the Royal Australian Navy in 1989 and was renamed **Westralia**. Comparison with the photograph at the top of the page reveals some detail differences.

(Russell Priest)

As the Hudson company moved away from ownership and into management, the range of vessels varied considerably. On this page we see two of the managed ships in Belgian waters. The tweendecker **Mostween 6** was photographed at in the River Scheldt at Antwerp on 4 May 1990.

(Leo van Ginderen collection, World Ship Photo Library)

The **Guyane** passes Terneuzen on her way up the River Scheldt on 15 April 2001.

(Tony Hogwood)

To close this colour section, we see two former Hudson vessels in the colours of subsequent owners. The 1958-built **Hudson Trader** was sold to Greek owners in 1973 after a little over two years in the Hudson fleet. She traded for four years as **Konstantinos G. Chimples** and was photographed as she approached Eastham.

(Bernard McCall)

The **Sonia 1** was photographed at Barry on 2 April 1989. Originally named **Hudson Light**, she was the first vessel in the fleet to have engines and all accommodation located aft.

(Bernard McCall)

Shortly after taking over **Moscliff**, Hudson Steamship was awarded the technical management of another tanker, **Stolidi**, for Maltese owners who had recently purchased the vessel. It was the intention of both parties to assess the management at the end of the year which in actual fact was terminated from 31 December 1993. During March 1994, **Stolidi** suffered a flash fire in her accommodation block which claimed the lives of twenty crew and she was later sold to Pakistani shipbreakers.

Mosvold's Annual Report for 1993 gave a gross operating income of NOK 54.9 million which included management fees and commissions of NOK 5.2 million and sales profit of NOK 1.9 million. The operating loss for the year was NOK 9 million with the vessels having a book value of NOK 274 million. Only **Moscliff** and **Mosdeep** were wholly-owned while a 10% ownership was held in **Mosriver**, **Mostween 5** and **Mostween 7**.

Throughout 1994, the company continued to manage five ships. **Mosdeep** remained on time charter to Fednav until June 1998 and **Moscliff** traded from the Persian Gulf to the Far East. Although placed on the spot market, the company was able to arrange individual voyage charters for **Moscliff** with Yukong Line, Seoul, South Korea. **Mostween 5** as mentioned obtained a time charter to Blue Star while **Mostween 7** traded predominantly in the Far East. **Mosriver** also spent the majority of the year on the spot market, although for a short period she went on time charter to Italmar SpA, Sorrento. In addition to the ships managed by Hudson Steamship, Mosvold chartered a Panamax bulk carrier, **Arkas**, for worldwide trading from October 1993 until September 1994. During 1994 the vessels which were operated earned a gross income of NOK 117 million for the Mosvold Group, the share of sales profits in the K/S companies totalled NOK 3 million. However, after depreciation the shipping operation returned a loss of NOK 8 million for the year which was on a par with the results of 1993.

In 1994, Mosvold Shipping A/S became the subject of a take-over from another Norwegian company. Mosvold was funded by two types of shares, A-shares allowing voting rights, B-shares which had no voting rights. In May 1994 Mosvold's Chairman, Mr Karl Mosvold and his relative Anton Ringoen purchased all the voting A-shares held by largest private shareholder, Bjarne Skeie. In September Karl Mosvold and Anton Ringoen sold the shares they now controlled to Oslo based B Skaugen Shipping A/S. Skaugen now owned 3,295,597 A-shares, equivalent to a 44.44% shareholding in Mosvold Shipping A/S. Under Norwegian law had they owned over 45% of the shares then they would have had to undertake a full take-over of Mosvold Shipping A/S.

Although experienced in shipping, Mosvold Shipping A/S had latterly diversified into offshore drilling, acquiring a 60% shareholding in an American company, Dual Drilling. As a result of two Extraordinary General Meetings held in November and December 1994, a new Board of Directors was appointed and the Articles of Association were rewritten. These now stated that the Mosvold shareholding in Dual Drilling would be sold and the proceeds distributed amongst the shareholders. However due to the depressed state of the drilling market it was not advisable to sell the shares in Dual and Mosvold continued to have a shareholding in the company.

During 1994 the Mosvold board considered the shipping markets with a view to shipping investments, presumably with the money raised from the sale of Dual Drilling. In their 1994 Annual Report, they concluded that the time was not right for an investment in shipping although the situation would be closely monitored. Apart from its shareholding in Mosvold Shipping A/S, B Skaugen Shipping A/S had a 60% shareholding in the ferry operator Color Line as well as owning or part owning a small number of tankers and bulk carriers.

In November 1994, **Mostween 5** and **Mosriver** were sold for further trading. **Mostween 5** was handed over at Singapore on 10 November, her new owners having sold her to Mosvold in 1989. Eight days later, **Mosriver** was handed over at Xingang, China to The Great Eastern Shipping Company, London, a subsidiary of the Indian shipping company of the same name. Hudson Steamship continued to manage **Mostween 7**, in which Mosvold had a 10% minority share.

Hudson Steamship's business remained unaffected by these changes to its parent company and continued to search for further ship management work. In 1994, Mosvold Shipping A/S, which was the holding company of the Mosvold group, transferred its shareholding in Thornhope Shipping Co Ltd to another subsidiary, Mosvold Shipping Ltd.

Mostween 5

(Tony Atkinson collection)

As a result of its contacts with Fednav through the time charter of **Mosdeep** and management of **Thekwini**, Hudson Steamship was awarded the management of two Capesize bulk carriers owned by Fednav. **Federal Skeena** and **Federal Hunter** came under the management of the company in 1995 and were both registered in Luxembourg. Both ships had been built in Belgium and were lengthened shortly after their completion. Their management had previously been with Belcan S A, Antwerp, formed by Fednav and the Belgium steel company Cockerill-Ougrée S A in 1967 to transport Canadian ore to Cockerill's steel plants. In 1991, both were transferred to the Luxembourg register retaining their Belgian managers. Hudson Steamship's management of these two vessels lasted only three weeks as Fednav informed Hudson Steamship on 2 May 1995 that it was selling the vessels to new owners.

Both vessels were sold in an en bloc deal to Louis Dreyfus & Cie, Paris. **Federal Skeena** was sale dry-docked in Rotterdam and handed over to her new owners on 22 May and renamed **La Cordillera** under the Panamanian flag. **Federal Hunter** was sold on 6 June, reportedly for $20 million, and renamed **Marine Hunter**. She was handed over at Palermo, although Dreyfus intended to resell her to a joint venture with a Turkish bulk carrier operator with delivery in South Korea during August 1995. Hudson Steamship remained the vessel's managers until she was handed over in South Korea.

In July 1995, Mosvold decided that it would disband its present shipmanagement operation, ie Hudson Steamship, and transfer the business, including its ISO/ISM Certification, to Norway. Mosvold would now centre its shipping activities in Oslo with the setting up of a small management team to look after **Moscliff** and **Mosdeep**. Rather than let this happen, Captain Davies persuaded Mosvold to let him try to find a buyer for Hudson Steamship.

Mosvold stated that it wished to have its shipping interests listed on the Oslo Stock Exchange by mid-November through a new Bermuda based subsidiary. A new company, Dual Invest, based in Oslo and the major shareholder in Dual Drilling would be created to look after Mosvold's offshore business, Mosvold ultimately intending to sell its interest in Dual Drilling. During this time, **Mostween 7** was sold to St Vincent & Grenadines owners for $3.5 million. Since January 1995, she had been on a nine month time charter and delivery to her new owners was scheduled for the end of her time charter in September, although due to circumstances she was not handed over until November. This in effect left Hudson Steamship with one ship to manage. Although Mosvold intended to takeover the management of both **Mosdeep** and **Moscliff**, Fednav objected to this move and insisted that management of **Mosdeep** remain with Hudson Steamship. Because of this, only **Moscliff** was taken over by Mosvold in late September 1995. Throughout her management, she had secured individual voyage charters from the Gulf to Korea, her average daily income being $12,100 on a 348 days trading basis, the vessel recording only 17 days off hire.

From November 1995 onwards, the company had only one ship to manage and many avenues were explored in the hope of finding new management contracts. Several companies had expressed an interest in Hudson Steamship but unfortunately nothing can come of these enquiries, the main problem being the liability of a longterm lease on Hudson Steamship's offices at 25 Ship Street, Brighton.

At the beginning of May 1996, Captain Davies was offered the opportunity of forming a new ship management company with the backing of two investors. The majority of Hudson Steamship office staff were offered, and accepted, positions with the new company, EuroShip Services Ltd, which was to be based at Purfleet on the Thames close to Dagenham Dock, the site of Hudson Steamship's origins through the Williams family.

Because most of the staff would leave the employment of Hudson Steamship on 30 May 1996, Mosvolds took the decision to place Hudson Steamship in a dormant state from that date. As of midnight on 31 May 1996, Australian time, **Mosdeep** was transferred to a Hong Kong ship management company. Towards the end of 1996, a sistership to **Moscliff** was purchased and renamed **Mosocean** under Thornhope ownership and in 1997 a further two VLCCs were also acquired. With this size of vessel commanding daily rates of $35,000 against daily costs of $11,000 they were an attractive proposition. In order to meet safety requirements, the ships were converted to segregated ballasting arrangements which would give them an added five years of trading.

Having completed seventy-six years in business as a ship owner and then manager Hudson Steamship saw many changes. Throughout its history it could best be described as a survivor. Having been created as a collier owning company its business diversified in the 1950/60s into a deep-sea company, owning two of the largest ships registered under the British flag. With the fall of the Williams Hudson Group it continued in business under the ownership of Lars Krogh where it was able to continue as a shipmanager, albeit in a reduced capacity. With its sale to Mosvold, Hudson Steamship enjoyed a renaissance, re-entering deep-sea trading with the management of some nineteen ships on behalf of the parent company and a number of ships for other owners employed worldwide. In August 1991 the company was accredited with the EN 29002-1987, ISO 9002-1987 and BS 5750 ship management quality awards followed in April 1995 by accreditation for compliance to the ISM code and in July the first vessel in the fleet was issued with an ISM safety management certificate. No company is guaranteed a future. Hudson Steamship had a small but experienced team which has since helped the new company to expand.

Finally on 1 October 1999, in a move reminiscent of the Sanhob deal, the identity of Hudson Steamship was swapped with that of another company, Hystona Ltd, which had been incorporated in 1997 and had its office in Nile Street, Brighton. The new Hudson Steamship Co Ltd was a short-lived venture and was dissolved on 15 August 2000, never having had a ship registered under its ownership. Two weeks previously, on 28 July, Hystona Ltd had been dissolved, thus ending the eighty-year history of Samuel Williams' Hudson Steamship Co Ltd.

BIBLIOGRAPHY

A Company's Story In its Setting Samuel Williams & Sons 1855 - 1955
The Williams Hudson Group Company Brochures,
The Williams Hudson Record, Group House Magazine
Welsh Blockade Runners in The Spanish Civil War - P M Heaton
Steam Coasters and Short Sea Traders - C V Waine
The Steam Collier Fleets - J A Mcrae & C V Waine
The Deep Sea Tramp - Capt G Course
Merchant Ships At War : The Falklands Experience - Capt R Villar,
The Royal Navy and The Falklands War - David Brown,
British Bulk Carriers 1945-1979 - I G Stewart, FCIS
British Gas Tankers & Gas Carriers 1955-1979 - I G Stewart FICS,
Twenty Tramp Fleets ,Vol 4 - N L Middlemiss
Saved from The Sea - Robert Malster
Also the following magazines and newspaper : *Ships Monthly, Sea Breezes, Marine News* (magazine of the World Ship Society), *South Shields Gazette, Sunderland Echo, Financial Times* for the period 1982 to 1988, *Lloyds Index Card Collection,* Guildhall Library London

With thanks to
Capt F Davies; Mr P K Arbuthnot; Mr J E Appleby; Mr A K Reynolds; Mr T Hall - former Managing Directors of Hudson SS Co Ltd; Mr A P Follett, former Superintendent, Hudson SS Co Ltd; the late Mr F White, former Personnel Manager Hudson Steamship Co Ltd; Mr R Bush, former Managing Director of John Hudson & Co Ltd; Mr J E Jones, former Secretary, Williams Hudson Group; Scottish Maritime Museum, Irvine; Cornwall Family History Society; Lloyd's Register of Shipping; Cammell Laird Shipbuilders; Newcastle City Library; Public Records Office, Kew; Andrew Breeden, Coventry; Capt O H Cook, Glasgow; World Ship Society Central Record Team, including Harold Appleyard (Billingham), Michael Crowdy (Kendal), David Burrell (Cumnock), Richard Osborne (Nailsea); special thanks to Gil Mayes for so much effort in checking the book; and to all the photographers who have loaned their valuable material. Finally, I must thank the staff of The Amadeus Press for bringing the finishing touches to the book.

APPENDIX 1

BBC Home Service, schools' broadcast; Thursday, 10 February 1966

In 1965, **Hudson Firth** featured in a BBC Radio schools programme about the transportation of coal from the north-east to the Thames. This is the transcript of the programme. Featured in the programme are Mr Philip Holland, the BBC reporter who sailed on **Hudson Firth**, Captain Tait, the ship's regular Master, and Captain Holliday one of the company's relieving masters who we believe acted as Mr Holland's guide for the trip.

****

Last week, you may remember, we learned something of how coal is mined at Bates Colliery in Northumberland, and how at the end of the programme, we saw coal being loaded into the ship **Hudson Firth**, which was lying in the River Blyth, alongside the colliery.

I made the voyage in the **Hudson Firth** from Northumberland to the Thames, and in this programme we shall hear something of what happened on the voyage.

Ships have been carrying coal from Northumberland to London at least since the 13th century, and probably since Roman times. In the year 1228, there was a street in London called Seal Coal Lane, and in 1369, four meters were built to measure the various cargoes of coal as they were unloaded from the ships. But it was during the 17th and 18th centuries, when the traditional fuel - wood - was no longer available in large quantities, because we had been cutting down so many of our forests that the coal trade from the north-east to the Thames began to boom. In 1575 to 1580, London was only using about 12,000 tons of coal a year - by 1800 the figure had risen to 455,000 tons.

The north-eastern coal fields were a popular source of supply for London, because both the coal fields and, of course, London itself had easy access to the sea, and so coal could be carried easily and cheaply along the east coast; and this is still true today. Bates Colliery is linked to the sea, a mile or two away, by the River Blyth, and ships can sail directly to the colliery to collect their cargoes.

Now most people, when they think of a collier, think of a dirty old ship, wallowing slowly along with worn out engines- the kind of ship that John Masefield described in his poem:-

"Dirty British coaster with a salt-caked smoke stack, butting down the Channel in the mad March days,
    With a cargo of Tyne coal, road rail, pig lead, firewood, ironware and cheap tin trays."

(Followed by the noise of the engines)

I quickly found, as the **Hudson Firth** sailed down the River Blyth and out into the North Sea, how things have changed since Masefield wrote those lines. For she's a modern ship of 4,000 tons - very smart and spotlessly clean, with separate cabins for each of the ship's crew, and all the latest aids to navigation. When I went out on to the bridge, for example, I found that there was no-one at the wheel - yet the ship was exactly on course. The ship was being steered, Captain Holliday told me, by an automatic helmsman, a gadget fixed to the top of the ship's compass, which held the ship on whatever course was required,and there were radar devices.

More and more ships nowadays carry radar as an aid to navigation, and the **Hudson Firth** is no exception. The scanner is mounted on top of the bridge the highest point on the ship,and the radar screen, - it's rather like a television screen - was on the bridge itself, close to the wheel.

CAPTAIN HOLLIDAY *This radar, of course, is for helping us along in hazy weather and we can tune it down to between .75 of a mile range, right up to near 25 miles, which, in practice, we hardly ever use. For ordinary use at sea, we generally keep it under six miles range and the rings on the screen are a mile apart. The scanner goes round and reflects the echoes of any object. At the present moment, we have one ship about two miles off our starboard beam, which we can see, the visibility being 5 miles anyway.*

Radar is especially necessary, of course, where shipping lanes are busy; the approaches to the Thames, for example, and along the whole of the east coast of England. If we leave out the Straits of Dover, where, of course, you see a great many ocean going ships as well as coasters, the east coast, from Northumberland to the Thames, is the busiest route for coastal vessels in the British Isles, and I haven't forgotten the route from Liverpool to Belfast. That is why, on the **Hudson Firth**, the officer of the watch kept a sharp eye on the radar screen, especially at night and in fog, but the most remarkable piece of equipment on the bridge was a small black box. Until quite recently the only way in which a sailor could find his position at sea if he was out of sight of land was with his sextant - this measured the angle of the sun, or at night of a star, from the horizon, and then, using a complicated series of tables, a sailor could work out his position. All this took time; of course, if the sun or the stars were hidden by cloud, then the sextant was useless.

The situation is very different nowadays with this small black box - a simple looking, but highly complex piece of electronic equipment, which gives the ship's exact position from moment to moment.

CAPTAIN HOLLIDAY *In simple language - to make sure that we can maintain our exact position on the chart with signals going out all the time, they are received by this black box by means of dials, the three lower dials relay the colours, which are red, green and purple to make a distinguishing mark.*

MR HOLLAND *Those are the different transmitting stations?*

CAPTAIN HOLLIDAY *Yes, and by the way we get the position through to us is by means of lattice charts, which are like a graph.*

MR HOLLAND *So where does that bring us now then?*

CAPTAIN HOLLIDAY *Our actual position is 2.5 miles, north-west of the Haisbro' Lightship, Haisbro' Sands.*

MR HOLLAND *And they are just off the coast of Norfolk?.*

CAPTAIN HOLLIDAY *Practically opposite to Cromer - between Cromer and Happisburgh.*

MR HOLLAND *How far off shore?.*

CAPTAIN HOLLIDAY *At the moment we are about 8 miles off the coast of Norfolk.*

All this time, the **Hudson Firth** was steaming south at a steady 10 knots - that's about 12 miles an hour. Off this part of the coast, I noticed a number of vessels, which were clearly oil tankers - though they were much smaller than the big ocean going tankers that come from the oil fields themselves. These coastal tankers were coming from refineries with oil products - petrol, diesel oil and so on. One of them, at least, looked as though it was heading for King's Lynn in Norfolk, where they have built a large storage depot - one of the many which have been built at convenient points between the Orkney Islands and Dover. The products these tankers carry are second only to coal in Britain's coastal trade, particulary on the east coast, where there are large refineries at the mouth of the Thames in the south, and in the north on the River Forth in Scotland.

Now you have only to measure the east coast on a map of the British Isles to see that some of the voyages made by the coastal vessels are fairly long. From Blyth, for example, some ships sail to the Channel Islands; then there is the journey from London to the Scottish ports, so that one of the most important men on the ship is the ship's cook, who has to order the food required for the voyage. The cook on board the **Hudson Firth** was John Clark, and I talked to him in what, on shore, would be called the kitchen, but at sea is called the galley. Mr Clark said that one popular dish was black pudding, and I asked him if there were any others.

JOHN CLARK *Tripe and onions is another popular dish from the north, you can say. Try and put it on with a Cockney crowd - you'll get the individual might like it, but not the crowd as a whole, you know. Pease pudding - things like that, you know - but they are all popular northern dishes really. Teas - well they have various teas - fish and chips, mince pies - things like that, you know - they are all pretty popular teas, you know - they go down pretty well.*

MR HOLLAND *Do you get any complaints?*

JOHN CLARK *Oh - you always get complaints - you'll never satisfy a ship's crew - never.*

There's certainly a lot of all-round experience to be gained on the coastal routes. I learned this in the engine room when I put a question about the ship's engines to Mr James Frazer, 2nd Engineer of the **Hudson Firth**. I asked him if the engines gave much trouble.

MR FRAZER. *Well you don't get a lot of trouble with it really. I mean to say, they are so reliable really if you keep looking after them. On this one now you can hear a knock. It will have to be a couple of liners taken out and adjusted a little more to stop that - otherwise, if you let it run too long, it hammers until it gets hot and the metal runs out, and, of course you have to worry about your work then. It means changing your bottom ends and putting spares on.*

MR HOLLAND *Would you carry spares aboard for a job like that?*

MR FRASER *We carry one spare bottom end.*

Amidships, under the bridge,I found the cabin of the Radio Operator, Brian Whittle. The tiny cabin was filled with radio transmitters and receivers, each duplicated in case of a breakdown. On the floor, by the door, was another large metal box painted bright yellow, and I asked Brian Whittle what it was.

MR WHITTLE *It's a lifeboat set you know. One man is supposed to carry it.*

MR HOLLAND *It's pretty big for one man to carry!*

MR WHITTLE *It's not too bad. It's a hand cranked machine that contains all the necessary distress frequencies; has an automatic tuning device for S.O.S. in case there is no radio officer in the lifeboat.*

MR HOLLAND *So, if the ship is sinking, what you are supposed to do is grab that before you go to the lifeboat?.*

MR WHITTLE *Yes - that's the idea.*

MR HOLLAND *Have you ever had to do that?*

MR WHITTLE *No! I haven't been sunk yet.*

We did, in fact, pick up two distress calls during the voyage - one from a Swedish ship whose cargo was on fire, and one from a French trawler, but in each case, other ships nearer than us were going to their help, and we heard later that both ships were continuing their voyage.

After the Master, the officer with the biggest responsibilities on board a ship is the First Mate. He is the second in command, and he is responsible to the Master for the running of the ship. I talked to the First Mate of the **Hudson Firth**, Mr R H Weatherly, whilst he was on watch on the bridge, and I asked him how long he had been in the coastal collier trade.

MR WEATHERLY *I have been about six months on the coast now, but before that I was deep sea for seven years.*

MR HOLLAND *What was it like coming on the coast?*

MR WEATHERLY *Strange - it takes a bit of time getting used to - the amount of traffic, and of course you pass ships much closer- and, of course, you work much harder. You work 4 hours on and 4 hours off all the time, whereas, deep sea, you work 4 hours on and 8 hours off. You have plenty of time for sleeping, or if you want to read or anything like that, you have got plenty of time.*

MR HOLLAND *And, of course, this coming into port every couple of days, does that mean more work?*

MR WEATHERLY *Oh yes, when you go into port, everybody has to be up on deck anyway, even if it's your 4 hours off, you still have to be up and out. Anyway, like tonight, half the watch below will have to be out on deck as well. I'll admit we make more money.*

MR HOLLAND *What about the navigating side of it?*

MR WEATHERLY   *Well, of course, on the coast, everything is done for you; no sights to work out - it's much easier as far as that goes. Then you have no long runs without seeing anything, and especially on this coal trade - if you don't know where you are, you just latch on to the one in front of you.*

And the one in front may, on the voyage north from the Thames, be a vessel carrying cement from the Medway towns of North Kent, perhaps to the Outer Hebrides. Cement is often a profitable return cargo for vessels which have, maybe, delivered coal or gravel to the ports in the south. Or the ship you are following north may be carrying scrap metal, also from the Medway to Middlesbrough. Scrap is big business nowadays; it is collected from all over the south of England, and sent by ship to the north-east, to be melted down and used again.

It was on the second night at sea that I talked to the Master of the **Hudson Firth** - Captain Geoffrey Tait. He was in his cabin getting ready to go up to the bridge, for the ship entering the Thames Estuary, which is one of the most crowded stretches of water in the world. Deeply loaded with coal as we were, it was important, not only that we should keep clear of other shipping, but also that we should follow the narrow, winding, deep water channel between the sandbanks on either hand. So my talk with Captain Tait had to be brief, but he did tell me how important it is, from the Master's point of view, to have a good crew.

CAPTAIN TAIT   *A good crew makes the job easier for the Master - there's no two ways about that. At sea you don't really have very much trouble, especially if you have a good Catering Dept. You don't get much trouble from the working conditions or anything - at least I haven't found so. In port, when the men get their subs and they get away for a few beers - that is usually when the trouble starts, but I think you will find modern seamen today are not like the old timers, where they hit port and they stopped ashore until it was time to sail or until their money was spent. Now, the average seaman today is more thrifty minded - he spends his money at home.*

Captain Tait told me that he had been in the coastal trade for more than 20 years. He prefers it to going abroad because he has more time for his family; but he also said, carrying coal to the Thames is very hard work, with short fast voyages and very little time in port.

Just what it means to be the Master of a collier, I learned in the next five hours, as I stood with Captain Tait on the bridge and watched him as he took his ship in the darkness of midnight up the estuary of the river. The darkness outside as we steamed slowly on was now alive with lights - lights of ships moving up and down the estuary - here, several miles wide; lights of buoys flashing white or red - once green lights, which marked a sunken ship lying in the channel; and, growing steadily closer, lights on shore, of factories, streets and houses, and I wondered how, in the darkness, Captain Tait could possibly follow the narrow twisting channel with such a confusion of lights around him. But, of course, he did and at 2 o'clock in the morning, he swung the ship gently alongside the floodlit jetty at Dagenham, on the northern shore of the Thames.

And so, after 32 hours at sea, the voyage ended. In a few hours time, at dawn, great mechanical grabs would unload the coal, either onto railway wagons or into barges, that would take it further up river, and that same afternoon, the **Hudson Firth** would be at sea again, on her way north for another 4,000 tons of coal.

So the collier trade to the Thames continues - every day; ships bringing thousands of tons of coal for the power stations and gas works; factories and fireplaces of London and southern England; coal from the Humber, from Blyth, from Tyneside, where the trade began so many years ago.

I think the writer - Horace Walpole - summed up very well how much we depend for our comfort on coal. One cold wet winter's day, when the sun seemed to have disappeared forever, he was sitting by a warm cosy fireside. This is what he wrote:- "The best sun we have is made of Newcastle coal". This ends today's programme in the Geography Series. The speaker was Phillip Holland and the broadcast was recorded.

Hudson Firth *heads south along the east coast of England, no doubt with another full cargo of coal for a Thames power station.*

(Skyfotos, author's collection)

VESSELS OWNED BY JOHN HUDSON & CO LTD, HUDSON STEAMSHIP CO LTD AND JOHN HUDSON FUEL AND SHIPPING LTD

1. *Oxshott*   1915 - 1941

O.N. 139035   1241 g   761 n   230.0' x 35.8' x 15.6'
T.3-cylinder engine by Rankin & Blackmore Ltd, Greenock

3.3.1915 : Launched by Campbeltown Shipbuilding Co Ltd, Campbeltown, (Yard No 100) for John Hudson & Co Ltd, London, as ***Oxshott***. 5.1915 : Completed. 13.4.1920 : Owners became Hudson Steamship Co Ltd, London. 6.8.1941: Ran aground on Haisborough Sands in a position 52.54.30N, 01.43.50E while on a voyage with coal from Seaham to Dagenham. Her master and four crew members were lost. She was one of seven merchant ships lost along with their escort, the anti-submarine trawler ***HMS Agate***, when in poor visibility and a NNW gale the signal to alter course was mis-read. She was later declared a total loss.

*This view of the **Oxshott** reveals the characteristic lines of vessels of her vintage.*

(Alex Duncan, WSPL)

2. *Hornchurch* (1)   1916 - 1917

O.N. 139154   2159 g   1301 n   280.0' x 40.0' x 18.5'
T.3-cylinder engine by Clyde Shipbuilding & Engineering Co Ltd, Port Glasgow

17.5.1916 : Launched by Osbourne, Graham & Co Ltd, Sunderland, (Yard No 200) for John Hudson & Co Ltd, London, as ***Hornchurch***. 9.1916 : Completed. 3.8.1917 : Sank 3.5 miles ENE of Coquet Island after she struck a mine, laid by the German submarine ***UC29***, when on a voyage from Methil to the Thames with coal. Two of her crew were lost.

3. *Upminster* (1)   1917 - 1928

O.N. 140255   2176 g   1272 n   280.0' x 40.5' x 18.5'
T.3-cylinder engine by Richardsons, Westgarth & Co Ltd, Sunderland

23.11.1916 : Launched by Osbourne, Graham & Co Ltd, Sunderland, (Yard No 201) for John Hudson & Co Ltd, London, as ***Upminster***. 3.1917 : Completed. 13.4.1920 : Owners became Hudson Steamship Co Ltd, London. 2.5.1928 : Sank after a collision with the steamer ***Lanrick*** (1283grt/20) off Flamborough Head while in ballast from London to Methil.

4. *Hornchurch* (2)   1919 - 1940

O.N. 143340   2162 g   1250 n   280.0' x 40.5' x 18.5'
T.3-cylinder engine by MacColl & Pollock Ltd, Sunderland

16.5.1919 : Launched by Osbourne, Graham & Co Ltd, Sunderland, (Yard No 258) for The Shipping Controller as ***War Browny***. 1919 : Acquired while fitting out by John Hudson & Co Ltd, London. 7.1919 : Completed as ***Hornchurch***. 13.4.1920 : Owners became Hudson Steamship Co Ltd, London. 12.7.1940 : While on a voyage with coal from Methil to London, she was attacked by German aircraft off Aldeborough Light Vessel in a position 52.11.15N 01.52.30E and later sank in a position 52.11.30N, 01.51.45E. Her crew of twenty-two were rescued.

A fine action photograph of the **Hornchurch** underway in ballast.

(Alex Duncan, WSPL)

5. *Dagenham*   1919 - 1956

O.N. 143424   2178g 1260n   280.0' x 40.5' x 18.5'
T.3-cylinder engine by MacColl & Pollock Ltd, Sunderland

13.8.1919 : Launched by Osbourne, Graham & Co Ltd, Sunderland, (Yard No 259) for The Shipping Controller, War Department, London, as **War Ness**. 1919 : Acquired by John Hudson & Co Ltd, London, while fitting out. 9.1919 : Completed as **Dagenham**. 13.4.1920 : Owners became Hudson Steamship Co Ltd, London. 16.11.1940 : Damaged by a mine 2.5 cables ENE of Mouse Light Vessel while on passage with coal from Methil to London and beached on Barrow Sands. 21.11.1940 : Refloated and beached at the Isle of Grain. 27.11.1940 : Refloated and towed to Dagenham where her cargo was discharged. She was repaired and returned to service approximately six months later. 9.4.1944 : Requisitioned for war service during Operation Neptune (Normandy Landings) and follow-up. 26.7.1945 : Returned to her owners. 1956: Sold to Minos Cia Maritima SA, Panama and renamed **Nikitas K**. 29.11.1957: Foundered off the Turkish Black Sea coast on a voyage from Stratoni to Braila with a cargo of pyrites. Eight of her crew of fourteen were saved.

The **Dagenham** moored to a buoy, possibly awaiting discharge in the Thames.

(Alex Duncan, WSPL)

6. *Lolworth*   1920 - 1940

O.N. 144509   1969g 1154n   270.0' x 40.2' x 17.2'
T.3-cylinder engine by North Eastern Marine Engineering Co Ltd, Sunderland

20.2.1920 : Launched by Osbourne, Graham & Co Ltd, Sunderland, (Yard No 220) for Hudson Steamship Co Ltd as **Lolworth**. It is believed she was ordered by The Shipping Controller, War Department, London, as **War Boyne** who sold her while on the slipway to John Hudson & Co Ltd, London. 4.1920 : Completed for Hudson Steamship Co Ltd, London. 10.2.1940 : Requisitioned as a naval collier by the Admiralty. 23.4.1940 : Mined and lost 1/2 mile NW off Elbow Light Buoy, off Broadstairs, while in ballast from Portsmouth to the Tyne. Two of her crew were lost.

7. *Upminster* (2)   1934 - 1940

O.N. 163538   1013g   576n   217.0' x 34.0' x 11.8'
T.3-cyliner engine by North Eastern Marine Engineering Co Ltd, Newcastle upon Tyne.

9.10.1934 : Launched by Burntisland Shipbuilding Co Ltd, Burntisland, (Yard No 183) for Hudson Steamship Co Ltd, London as *Upminster*. 11.1934 : Completed. 9.1.1940 : While on passage from Methil to London with 1,350 tons of coal, she was attacked by German aircraft about 9 miles SE of Hammond Knoll Light Vessel. 10.1.1940 : Sank in a position 53.03N 01.29E with the loss of her Master and two crew.

8. *Brasted*   1938 - 1945

O.N. 166344   1076g   605n   223.4' x 34.0' x 11.9'
T.3-cylinder engine by North Eastern Marine Engineering Co Ltd, Newcastle upon Tyne

16.12.1937 : Launched by Burntisland Shipbuilding Co Ltd, Burntisland, (Yard No 217) for Hudson Steamship Co Ltd, London, as *Brasted*. 1.1938 : Completed. 1945 : Sold to Onesimus Dorey & Sons Ltd, Guernsey. 1946 : Renamed *Belgrave*. 1962 : Sold to Van Heyghen Frères for demolition. 9.3.1962 : Arrived Ghent

*Official builder's cards of the **Upminster** and **Brasted**.*   *(WSPL)*

9. *Bramhill*   1941 - 1946

O.N. 145645   1921g   1090n   264.0' x 39.0' x 16.9'
T.3-cylinder engine by North Eastern Marine Engineering Ltd, Sunderland.

14.6.1923 : Launched by Robert Thompson & Sons Ltd, Sunderland, (Yard No 319) for Mordey Son & Co Ltd, Newport, as *Gwentland*. 7.1923 : Completed. 1936 : Sold to Bramhill Steamship Co Ltd (Angel, Dalling & Co Ltd, managers), Cardiff, for £10,250 and renamed *Bramhill*. 1938 : Owners became Angel, Son & Co Ltd, Cardiff. 1941 : Acquired by Hudson Steamship Co Ltd, London, for £40,000. 3.5.1944 : Requisitioned for war service in Operation Neptune (Normandy Landing) and follow-up during which time she suffered extensive damage. 8.12.1944 : Returned to her owners. 1946 : Sold to Shamrock Shipping Co Ltd (William C Lawson, managers), Larne, and renamed *Slemish*. 1950 : Managers became C S Brown, Larne. 1955 : Sold to Thos. Leitch (Shipping) Ltd, London. 9.3.1956 : Beached in a sinking condition in the River Thames after a collision with the steamer *Borde* (3401grt/53) while inward from the Tyne to Rotherhithe with coal. 12.4.1956 : Refloated near Littlebrook. Declared a constructive total loss and sold to BISCO; allocated to T W Ward Ltd, Sheffield. 7.5.1956 : Arrived Grays, Essex, for demolition. (Note : she was to have been renamed *Elenel* by her new owners, but this had not taken place at the time of the collision.)

*The **Bramhill** is seen here when named **Slemish**. The landscape in the background suggests that she is making her way cautiously up the River Thames.*

(WSPL)

10. *Macbrae*   1941 - 1949

O.N. 147934   2117g   1236n   274.5' x   39.9' x   23.3'
T3-cylinder engine by D Rowan & Co Ltd, Glasgow

14.10.1924 : Launched by Burntisland Shipbuilding Co Ltd, Burntisland, (Yard No 132) for Grahamston Shipping Co Ltd, Glasgow, (T L Duff & Co, managers), as *Carlbeath*. 12.1924 : Completed.   1937 : Sold to Guardian Line Ltd, Cardiff, (C A Roberts, managers) for £32,500 and renamed *Macbrae*. 1941 : Acquired by Hudson Steamship Co Ltd, London. 1949 : Sold to J B Shipping Co Ltd, Middlesbrough, (H P Marshall & Co Ltd, managers) and renamed *Ayton*. 1956 : Sold to Compania Isla de Oro Ltda, Panama, and renamed *Ange*. 1958 : Sold to Mediterranean Shipping Comp Inc, Panama, and renamed *Alcyone*. 24.8.1958 : Grounded and abandoned NE of Cape Sidheros, Northern Crete, after a fire broke out while on a voyage from Split to Aden with a cargo of cement. 25.8.1958 : Fire extinguished. 28.8.1958 : Refloated and towed to Piraeus. After being laid up at Perama, she was declared a constructive total loss and broken up locally.

The *Macbrae* leaves behind a fine trail of smoke.

(Author's collection)

A much better photograph of the *Macbrae* when she was named *Ayton* and owned in Middlesbrough.

(George Scott)

11. *Philipp M*   1942 - 1944

O.N. 147908   2085g   1239n   247.5' x   39.9' x   23.3'
T.3-cylinder engine by D Rowan & Co Ltd, Glasgow

19.4.1924 : Launched by Burntisland Shipbuilding Co Ltd, Burntisland, (Yard No 128) for Grahamston Shipping Co Ltd Glasgow, (T L Duff & Co, managers), as *Halbeath*. 12.1924 : Completed. 1937 : Sold to Mooringwell SS Co Ltd, Cardiff, for £32,500 and renamed *Philipp M*. 1942 : Acquired by Hudson Steamship Co Ltd, London, for £54,000. 24.2.1944 : Torpedoed and sunk near Hearty Knoll off Great Yarmouth by an E-boat with the loss of seven crew, including her Master. She was on passage from the Tyne to London with 3,102 tons of coal.

A rare photograph of the short-lived *Philipp M*.

(John Ives collection)

12. *Hetton*   1944 - 1946

O.N. 148068   2659g   1560n   308.0' x   44.0' x   20.8'
T.3-cylinder engine by North Eastern Marine Engineering Co Ltd, Sunderland.

1.5.1924 : Launched by S P Austin & Son Ltd, Sunderland (Yard No 305) for Tanfield Steamship Co Ltd, Newcastle, as *Hetton*. 1924 : Completed. 1933 : Managers became W B Nisbet, Newcastle upon Tyne. 7.9.1940 : Sustained bomb damage during an air raid while moored in the Pool of London. 1944 : Acquired by Hudson Steamship Co Ltd, London. 16.9.1944 : Requisitioned for war service in Operation Neptune (Normandy Landings) and follow-up. 28.9.1944 : Returned to the company. 1946 : Sold to Chang Kee Steamship Co Ltd, Tsingtao, China, and renamed *Heng Chun*. 1954 : Sold to Eddie Steamship Co Ltd, Taipeh, Formosa, and renamed *Polly*. 3.1958 : Reported to have been broken up.

*The **Hetton** seen from the classic three-quarter bow angle almost at water level.*

(George Scott)

13. *Empire Lagoon* / *Hudson Bay*   1945 - 1964

O.N. 168792   2013g 1083n   272.0' x 40.0' x 17.2'
T.3-cylinder engine by North Eastern Marine Engineering Co (1938) Ltd, Newcastle upon Tyne.

15.3.1941 : Launched by Grangemouth Dockyard Co Ltd, Grangemouth, (Yard No 433) for The Ministry of War Transport (F L Dawson & Co Ltd, Newcastle upon Tyne, managers) as *Empire Lagoon*. 6.1941 : Completed. 1942 : Managers became Hudson Steamship Co Ltd, London. 26.11.1945 : Acquired by Hudson Steamship Co Ltd, London, under the Ship Disposal Scheme. 1946 : Renamed *Hudson Bay*. 3.1964 : Sold to Hughes Bolckow Ltd for demolition at Blyth having been laid up there for some time. 9.3.1964 : Moved from her lay up berth to the breaker's yard.

*The first engine-aft vessel in the Hudson fleet, the **Hudson Bay** outward bound in the Thames.*

(WSPL)

14. *Hudson Bank*   1946 - 1959

O.N. 167648   2076g 1085n   272.0' x 40.2' x 17.2'
T.3-cylinder engine by Ailsa Shipbuilding Co Ltd, Troon. 1959 : Re-engined with a 7-cylinder 4SA oil engine by Machinenfabrik Augsberg-Nurnberg AG, Augsberg, West Germany.

10.11.1942 : Launched by Ailsa Shipbuilding Co Ltd, Troon, (Yard No 443) for The Ministry of War Transport (Wm Cory & Sons Ltd, London, managers) as *Empire Pioneer*. 12.1942 : Completed. 1944 : Managers became Hudson Steamship Co Ltd, London. 2.1946 : Acquired by Hudson Steamship Co Ltd under the Ship Disposal Scheme and renamed *Hudson Bank*. 1959 : Sold to Ertel Reederei GmbH, Hamburg and renamed *Gertrud C. Ertel*. 1959 : Re-engined. 1964 : Sold to Deutsch-Nordische Schiffahrtsges mbH, Hamburg, and renamed *Saga*. 24.12.1965 : Grounded during bad weather off Falsterbo, southern Sweden, while on a voyage with coal from Klaipeda to France and was abandoned by her crew who were taken off by a pilot boat the following day. 3.1.1966 : Broke in two and later declared a constructive total loss. 7.1968 : Refloated. 29.7.1968 : Arrived at Oskarshamn where 3,152 tonnes of coal was salved. 8.1968 : Sold to Aktiebolaget Oskarshamns Varv, Sweden, for demolition and broken up by them at Oskarshamn.

A threequarter stern view of the ***Hudson Bank****.*

(Tom Rayner, author's collection)

15. *Hudson Strait*   1946 - 1967

O.N. 180971   3105g 1687n   325.5' x 44.7' x 20.5'
T.3-cylinder engine by Ailsa Shipbuilding Co Ltd, Troon

27.6.1946 : Launched by Ailsa Shipbuilding Co Ltd, Troon, (Yard No 461) for Hudson Steamship Co Ltd, London, as *Hudson Strait*. 10.1946 : Completed. 1967 : Sold to Pargomar SA, Panama (Francesco Riviecco, Torre del Greco, Italy, managers) and renamed *Carmelina*. 1975 : Sold to Giuseppe Riccardi, Italy, for demolition. 25.11.1975 : Work commenced at Vado Ligure.

The oil tanks at Canvey Island form the backdrop to the ***Hudson Strait*** *as she makes her up the Thames.*   *(WSPL)*

16. *Hudson Cape*   1946 - 1966

O.N. 181551   2524g 1361n 3561d
293.5' x 42.3' x 18.9'
T.3-cylinder engine by Ailsa Shipbuilding Co Ltd, Troon.

24.10.1946 : Launched by Ailsa Shipbuilding Co Ltd, Troon, (Yard No 460) for Hudson Steamship Co Ltd, London, as *Hudson Cape*. 12.1946 : Completed. 1966 : Sold to E H Maritime Poseidon Ltd, (G E Houry & Son Ltd, London, managers), renamed *Eugenie* and transferred to Cyprus flag 1970 : Sold to Marittima Fresno SA, Honduras. 1971 : Sold to Brodospas, Yugoslavia, for demolition and arrived at their yard at Split on 18.3.1971.

Hudson Cape in the Thames estuary with another cargo of coal.
(Alex Duncan, WSPL)

17. *Hudson River*   1949 - 1973

O.N. 183094   3128g 1659n   325.5' x 44.7' x 20.5'
T.3-cylinder engine by Ailsa Shipbuilding Co Ltd, Troon

28.4.1949 : Launched by Ailsa Shipbuilding Co Ltd, Troon, (Yard No 466) for Hudson Steamship Co Ltd, London, as *Hudson River*. 8.1949 : Completed. 1973 : Sold to Sea Channel SA, (Adamitron Ltd, Rayleigh, managers), renamed *Ive* and transferred to Panama flag. 1976 : Sold to Desguaces y Salvamentos SA, Spain, for demolition. 6.10.1976 : Work began at San Juan de Nieva, Aviles.

As noted on page 13, there were several differences between the Hudson River, seen in the photograph on the right, and the Hudson Firth in the lower photograph.

(WSPL)

18. *Hudson Firth*   1949 - 1967

O.N. 183158   3117g 1659n   325.5' x 44.7' x 20.5'
T.3-cylinder engine by Ailsa Shipbuilding Co Ltd, Troon

8.9.1949 : Launched by Ailsa Shipbuilding Co Ltd, Troon, (Yard No 467) for Hudson Steamship Co Ltd, London, as *Hudson Firth*. 12.1949 : Completed. 1967 : Sold to Cia Naviera Rivabella SA, Panama, and renamed *Lugano*. 1972 : Sold to W H Arnott Young & Co Ltd for demolition. 11.10.1972 : arrived at Dalmuir from Birkenhead. 15.12.1972 : Work commenced.

19. *Hudson Sound* (1)   1950 - 1967

O.N. 184338   2577g 1355n
292.6' x 42.2' x 19.1'
T.3-cylinder engine by Ailsa Shipbuilding Co Ltd, Troon

27.9.1950 : Launched by Ailsa Shipbuilding Co Ltd, Troon, (Yard No 469) for Hudson Steamship Co Ltd, London, as *Hudson Sound*. 12.1950 : Completed. 1967: Sold to Darien Shipping Co Inc, Panama (Southern Shipping Co Inc, New Orleans, managers) and renamed *Rosella*. 1970 : Sold to Gulf Navigation Corporation, and renamed *Cathy* under the Panama flag. 1971 : Sold to Old Dominion Maritime Corporation, Panama (Adler, Gross & Thaler, New York, managers) and renamed *Vedalin*. 1973 : Sold to Aguilar y Peris, Spain, for demolition. 20.8.1973 : Arrived at Burriana from Baltimore where she had been laid up since 5.2.1973. Work commenced during 9.1973.

Moored to buoys fore and aft, the **Hudson Sound** *may be awaiting her turn to discharge, but the snow covering on the hatch covers and other parts of the ship could indicate that the collier was laying by over the Christmas period.*

(WSPL)

20. *Hudson Deep* (1)   1952 - 1972

O.N. 184688   6197g 3401n   416.0' x 55.7' x 28.8'
4-cylinder 2SA oil engine by North Eastern Marine Engineering Co (1938) Ltd, Wallsend

23.4.1952 : Launched by John Readhead & Sons Ltd, South Shields, (Yard No 570) for Hudson Steamship Co Ltd, London, as *Hudson Deep*. 8.1952 : Completed. 1972 : Sold to Rodosea Shipping Co Ltd, (Tsakos Shipping & Trading SA, Piraeus, managers), renamed *Irenes Hope* and transferred to Cyprus flag. 13.12.1978 : Sank in an approximate position 32.46N 28.15E, NW of Alexandria after a sea valve had fractured the previous day while she was on a voyage with general cargo from Civitavecchia to Dammam. Her crew were rescued and landed at Kalilimenes, southern Crete.

Possibly dropping her river pilot, the **Hudson Deep** *makes slow progress as she leaves the Thames.*

(Alex Duncan, WSPL)

21. **Hudson Point**   1957 - 1966

O.N. 187521   7863 g   4313 n   10450 d   475' 3" x 61' 0" x 25'10½"
4-cylinder 2SA oil engine by William Doxford & Sons (Engineering) Ltd, Sunderland

4.10.1956 : Launched by John Readhead & Sons Ltd, South Shields, (Yard No 590) for Hudson Steamship Co Ltd, London, as **Hudson Point**. 1.1957 : Completed. 1966 : Sold to China Shipping Co Ltd, Hong Kong, (John Manners & Co Ltd, Hong Kong, managers) and renamed **East Breeze**. 1967 : Owners became Compass Shipping Co Ltd, Hong Kong, (John Manners & Co Ltd, Hong Kong, managers). 1967 : Owners became Pacific Shipping & Enterprises Corporation (John Manners & Co Ltd, Hong Kong, managers), renamed **San Roberto** and transferred to Panama flag. 1974 : Sold to Fodele Shipping Co Ltd, Piraeus, and renamed **Fodele II** (Cyprus flag). 1979 : Sold to Argentine shipbreakers. 9.11.1979 : arrived in tow at Campana from San Nicholas for breaking up.

*The grey-hulled **Hudson Point** was the largest vessel in the fleet when she entered service in 1957.*

(J Y Freeman / Russell Priest)

22. **Hudson Light**   (1965 - 1976)

O.N. 307885   5628g   2842n   8442d   369' 7" x 53' 6" x 23' 5¾"
4-cylinder 2SA oil engine by William Doxford & Sons (Engineers) Ltd, Sunderland

5.4.1965 : Launched by John Readhead & Sons Ltd, South Shields, (Yard No 616) for Hudson Steamship Co Ltd, London, as **Hudson Light**. 7.1965 : Completed. 1966 : Owners became John Hudson Fuel & Shipping Ltd.1971 : Managers became Hudson Steamship Co Ltd, London. 1976 : Sold to the Central Electricity Generating Board, London, (Hudson Steamship Co Ltd, London, managers) and renamed **Castle Point**. 1978 : Managers became Christian Salvesen (Shipping) Ltd, Leith. 17.3.1986 : Laid up at Hartlepool. 1988 : Sold to Venetton United Corporation, (Socomar SrL, Naples, managers) and renamed **Sonia I** (Panama flag). 1989 : Sold to Sonia Maritime Co Ltd, Malta (PPA Professional Partners SA, Lugano, managers) and renamed **Shane** (Malta flag). 1996 : Transferred to the Belize Register. 1996 : Sold to Solid Shipping S.A., (Interline Gemicilik ve Dis Ticaret, Sirketi, Istanbul, managers) and renamed **Kaan** (Belize flag). 30.12.1998 : When on a voyage from Turkey to Spain with cement and iron ore, suffered a fire off Siracusa in a position 36.40N 14.53E and was abandoned by her crew. The fire was extinguished the following day and she arrived prior to 21.1.1999 at Pozzallo where she was declared a constructive toal loss. One crew member subsequently died of his injuries. 1999 : Sold to Turkish shipbreakers. 3.3.1999 : arrived at Aliaga for demolition.

*With engine and all accommodation located aft, the **Hudson Light** presented another new profile in the Hudson fleet.*

(J K Byass)

JH1. **Bel-Hudson**   1968 - 1976

O.N. 336912   15836g 9261n 24340d   591' 7" x 75' 2" x 33' 5³/₄"
7-cylinder 2SA Burmeister & Wain oil engine by A/S Akers M/V, Oslo, Norway

9.5.1968 : Launched by Kaldnes Mek. Verkstad A S, Tonsberg, Norway (Yard No 178) for Georg Vefling, Tonsberg, Norway, as **Belveni**. 1968 : Acquired for £2.2 million while fitting out to John Hudson Fuel & Shipping Ltd, London, and renamed **Bel-Hudson**. 1968 : Completed by Blohm & Voss AG, Hamburg, West Germany, where she was fitted with dual capacity for use as a car carrier and bulk carrier. 1971 : Managers became Hudson Steamship Co Ltd, London, until 1973. 1976 : Sold to Dampskips A/S Laly, (C T Gogstad & Co, Oslo, managers) and renamed **Leal** (Norway flag). 1980 : Sold to Mersina Shipping Co Ltd, (Tsakos Shipping & Trading SA, Piraeus, managers) and renamed **Irenes Zeal** (Greece flag). 1986 : Sold to Imola Shipping Co Ltd, (Tiddles Co Ltd, Hong Kong, managers) and renamed **Serene** (Cyprus flag). 1986 : Sold to Mainland Chinese shipbreakers. 5.8.1986 : sailed from Inchon. 7.8.1986 : arrived Qinhuangdao for demolition.

The impressive array of cargo handling gear is evident in this view of the **Bel-Hudson** underway in ballast.

(J K Byass)

JH2. **Hudson Trader**   1970 - 1973

O.N. 338952   12617g 7121n 19000d   559' 8" x 72' 0" x 30' 3"
6-cylinder 2SA oil engine made by William Doxford & Sons (Engineers) Ltd, Sunderland

22.10.1957 : Launched by J L Thompson & Sons Ltd, Sunderland, (Yard No 694) for Westfal Larsen & Co A/S, Bergen, Norway, as **Spinanger**. 2.1958 : Completed. 1970 : Acquired by John Hudson Fuel & Shipping Ltd, London. 1971 : Renamed **Hudson Trader**. 1971 : Managers became Hudson Steamship Co Ltd, London. 1973 : Sold to Andros Trading Ltd, Greece, (Affiliated Shipping Agency Inc, Cleveland, Ohio, managers) and renamed **Konstantinos G. Chimples**. 1977 : Renamed **Pelineon**. 1978 : Sold to Love Shipping Services Inc, Greece, (Universal Glow Inc Piraeus, managers) and renamed **Toplou Bay**. 1979 : Sold to Skopelos Shipping Corporation, (Eletson Shipping Corporation, Piraeus, managers) and renamed **Skopelos** (Greece flag). 1983 : Sold to Astakos Shipping Co SA, Greece, (Zoulias Brothers & Co, Piraeus, managers) and renamed **Theodosia V**. 1983 : Sold to Varela Davalillo, Spain, for demolition. 2.5.1983 : arrived at Castellon. 23.5.1983 : demolition began.

The **Hudson Trader** exemplifies the design of very many handy-sized tankers built during the 1950s. These were multi-purpose vessels able to carrry black oils or cleaner products. When bought by the Hudson group, it was expected that she would carry clean products but her poor condition made this difficult.

(J K Byass)

JH4. **Hudson Stream**   1971 - 1972

O.N. 341250   1330g 678n 1892d   238' 8" x 42' 9" x 12' 6"
After 1.1974   1555g 797n 2400d   271' 4" x 55' 10" x 15' 5"
2 x 8-cylinder 4SA oil engines by Lister Blackstone Mirrlees Marine, Dursley.

11.12.1970 : Launched by A Vuyk & Zonen's Scheepsbouwwverven NV, Capelle a/d IJssel, Holland, (Yard No 853) for John Hudson Fuel & Shipping Ltd, (Hudson Steamship Co Ltd, London, managers) as **Hudson Stream**. 3.1971 : Completed. 1972 : Sold to British Dredging (Sand & Gravel) Ltd, Cardiff, converted to a sand dredger and renamed **Bowstream**. 21.11.1973 : Sank in River Oude Maas, near Dordrecht, after she was in collision with the inland waterways vessel **Krammer**. She was later raised and extensively rebuilt and lengthened. 1977 : Owners became British Dredging Aggregates Ltd, London. 1979 : Owners became British Dredging (Sand & Gravel) Ltd, London. 1984 : Owners became East Coast Aggregates Ltd, Romford. 1990 : Owners became South Coast Shipping Co Ltd, Southampton. 1991 : Owners became East Coast Aggregates Ltd (South Coast Shipping Co Ltd, Southampton, managers). 1995 : Sold to Seal Sands Maritime Ltd, (Bilberry Shpg & Stevedores Ltd, Bilberry, County Waterford, managers). 1997 : Sold to Antonio Pereira e Filhos Ltd, Funchal, Madeira, and renamed **Porto Nova** and transferred to the St Vincent & Grenadines register.

Another fine view of the **Hudson Stream** provided specially for this book by the builders of the vessel.

(A Vuyk & Zonen's Scheepsbouwwerven NV, courtesy Bert Kruidhof)

JH4. *Hudson Venture*   1971 - 1976

O.N. 341414
125,310g 107,796n 254,520d
356,22m (inc BB) x 51,87m x 20,073m
2 x Stal Laval steam turbines, single reduction
geared to single shaft by Kockums Mekaniska
Verkstads A/B, Malmö.

25.4.1971 : Launched by Kockums Mekaniska
Verkstads A/B, Malmö, Sweden, (Yard No 526) for
John Hudson Fuel & Shipping Ltd, London,
(Hudson Steamship Co Ltd, London, managers
until 1973), as *Hudson Venture*. 1971 :
Completed. 1976 : Sold to R/A Trajan, Bergen,
(Hilmar Reksten, Bergen, managers) and renamed
Gratian. 1979 : Managers became Rederi-A/S
Johan Reksten, Fossanger. 1983 : Sold to China
Dismantled Vessels Corporation, Taiwan, for
demolition. 28.3.1983 : Arrived at Kaohsiung for
demolition by Lung Fa & Iron Co Ltd. 13.4.83 :
Work commenced. 16.5.1983 : Work completed.

Hudson Venture

(J K Byass)

JH5. *Hudson Friendship*   1971 - 1976

O.N. 342862   125,310g 107,797n 254,520d   356,22m (inc BB) x 51,85m x 20,073m
2 x Stal Laval steam turbines, single reduction geared to a single shaft by Kockums Mekaniska Verkstads A/B, Malmö.

3.7.1971 : Launched by Kockums Mekaniska Verkstads A/B, Malmö, Sweden, (Yard No 527) for John Hudson Fuel and
Shipping Ltd, London (Hudson Steamship Co Ltd, managers until 1973) as *Hudson Friendship*. 9.1971 : Completed.
1976 : Sold to Rederi-A/S Trajan, Norway, (Hilmar Reksten Rederi-A/S, Bergen, managers), and renamed *Gordian*.
1979 : Managers became Rederi-A/S Johan Reksten, Fossanger. 1979 : Sold to Neste O/Y, Finland (Rederiet Johan
Reksten, Naantali, managers until 1981) and renamed *Jatuli*. 1982 : Sold to St. Tobias Shipping Co, (Fearnley & Eger
A/S, Oslo, managers) and renamed *St Tobias* (Liberia flag).   11.9.1984 : Struck by an Iraqi airborne missile
approximately 50 miles south of Kharg Island in a position 28.5'N, 50.25'E while on a voyage from Kharg Island to Ube,
Japan. The missile hit a starboard ballast tank but did not cause a fire and the vessel berthed at Fujairah for inspection
before proceeding to Japan to discharge her cargo. 18.10.1984 : Sailed from Yokohama after being sold to mainland
Chinese shipbreakers.   Prior to 31.12.1984 : Arrived at Dalian Shipyard, Dalian, where she was broken up in the
graving dock.

An impressive trials view of the **Hudson Friendship**.
(Builder's photograph in company archives)

JH6. *Hudson Progress*　　1975

O.N. 386245　　　　19976g　13642n　33751d　　　　170,69m (inc B.B.)　x　25,94m　x　11,861m
2 x 14-cylinder 4SA Pielstick Vee oil engines each single reduction geared to a single screw by Crossley Premier Engines Ltd, Manchester

12.2.1975 : Launched by Cammell Laird Shipbuilders Ltd, Birkenhead, (Yard No 1362) for John Hudson Fuel & Shipping Ltd, London, as *Hudson Progress*. 7.1975 : Completed and laid up on the Mersey after her owners refused delivery. 1976 : Owners became Moonchase Ltd, a subsidiary company of the builders. 1979 : Sold to Lloyds Industrial Leasing Ltd, London, subsequently leased to Parley Augustson, Norway, and renamed *Balder London*. 6.5.1982 : Requisitioned for service during the Falklands conflict, and returned to civilian service at the end of hostilities. 9.3.1984 : Arrived at Falmouth for conversion to a replenishment tanker for bareboat charter to The Ministry of Defence (Navy). 2.5.1984 : Commissioned at Falmouth as *Orangeleaf*. 1995 : Managers became Government of The United Kingdom (The Secretary of State for Defence) (Commodore Royal Fleet Auxiliary), Portsmouth. 2000 : Managers became Government of the United Kingdom (Ministry of Defence - Ship Support Agency). 2001 : Sold to Government of The United Kingdom (Commodore Royal Fleet Auxiliary, Portsmouth, managers), London.

JH7. *Hudson Cavalier*　　1976

O.N. 388145　　　　19975g　13641n　33945d　　　　170,69m (inc B.B.)　x　25,96m　x　11,864m
2 x 14-cylinder 4SA Pielstick Vee oil engines, each single reduction geared to a single screw by Crossley Premier Engines Ltd, Manchester.

24.7.1975 : Launched by Cammell Laird Shipbuilders Ltd, Birkenhead, (Yard No 1363) for John Hudson Fuel & Shipping Ltd, London, as *Hudson Cavalier*. 12.1976 : Completed and laid up on the Mersey after her owners refused delivery. 1976 : Owners became Mastlake Ltd, a subsidiary company of the builders. 10.12.1978 : Arrived Wallsend for conversion to a replenishment tanker for bareboat charter to the Royal Fleet Auxiliary. 9.1979 : Sold to Matheson & Co Ltd, London, (Indo China Steam Navigation Co, [Hong Kong] Ltd, Hong Kong, managers, until 1983), and renamed *Appleleaf*. 11.4.1982 : Took part in the Falklands conflict until 25.7.1982. 1989 : Sold to Government of the Commonwealth of Australia (Department of Defence), (Dawson Industries Ltd, Perth, Western Australia, managers). 27.9.1989 : Commissioned at Immingham as *Westralia*. 5.5.1998 : Seriously damaged by an engine room fire while taking part in an exercise off Rotnest Island, Western Australia. As a result of the fire, four crew were killed and nine were injured and the vessel lost power as the fire took 1½ hours to extinguish. 1999 : Managers became Brown & Root Engineering Pty Ltd, Perth, Western Australia. 22.11.1999 : Completed contractors' sea trials off the west Australian coast following an $Australian 8.3m refit by Australian Defence Industries Ltd having spent 19 months alongside at *HMAS Stirling* which included safety modifications and onboard configurational changes. 2001 : Managers became Australian Defence Industries (ADI) Ltd, Rockingham, Western Australia.

Hudson Cavalier (left) and *Hudson Progress* (below) laid up in Liverpool.

(both Torsten Andreas)

JH8. *Hudson Deep* (2)

O.N. 388293   20440g 10680n 33257d   170,69m (inc B.B.) x 27,18m x 11,864m
2 x 14-cylinder 4SA Pielstick Vee oil engines, each single reduction geared to a single screw by Crossley Premier
Engines Ltd, Manchester.

22.1.1976 : Launched by Cammell Laird Shipbuilders Ltd, Birkenhead (Yard No 1365) for John Hudson Fuel & Shipping
Ltd, London, as *Hudson Deep*. While the vessel was fitting out her owners refused delivery. Upon completion she was
laid up on the Mersey. 1976 : Owners became Oakspine Ltd, a subsidiary company of the builders. 12.1978 : Work
began by her builders to convert her to a replenishment tanker for bareboat charter to the Royal Fleet Auxiliary.
2.1980 : Sold to Finance for Shipping Ltd, (Matheson & Co Ltd, London, managers), and renamed *Brambleleaf*. 1982 :
Took part in the Falklands conflict. 1983 : Sold to Matheson & Co Ltd, London. 1983 : Sold to the Government of the
United Kingdom (Director General of Supplies & Transport [Naval], Ministry of Defence [Navy], managers). 1995 :
Managers became Government of the United Kingdom (The Secretary of State for Defence) (Commodore Royal Fleet
Auxiliary), Portsmouth). 2000 : Managers became the Government of the United Kingdom (Ministry of Defence - Ship
Support Agency, Portsmouth). 2001 : Owners became the Government of the United Kingdom (Commodore Royal
Fleet Auxiliary, Portsmouth, managers), London.

Hudson Deep laid up at Liverpool.

(Bernard McCall)

Now named *Brambleleaf*, the same
tanker fully fitted out as a Royal Fleet
Auxiliary is seen approaching Portsmouth.

(WSPL)

JH9. *Yard No. 1366 / Hudson Sound* (2)

O.N.399072   20439g 10680n 29999d   170,69m (inc B.B.) x 25,94m x 11,861m
2 x 14-cylinder 4SA Pielstick Vee oil engines, each single reduction geared to a single screw by Crossley Premier
Engines Ltd, Manchester

14.2.1975 : Keel laid by Cammell Laird Shipbuilders Ltd, Birkenhead, as Yard No 1366, for John Hudson Fuel &
Shipping Ltd, London, and allocated the name *Hudson Sound*. 1976 : When John Hudson Fuel & Shipping Ltd
refused delivery, work, which was at an early stage, was halted. 1976 : Owners became Bluecross Ltd, a subsidiary
company of the builders. The small amount of work that had been undertaken was removed to storage, the builders
stating that should an order for a tanker be forthcoming the parts in storage would be used. 1980 : The Royal Fleet
Auxiliary ordered a replenishment tanker from Cammell Laird Shipbuilders Ltd, Birkenhead, for charter from civilian
owners. 12.1980 : Work restarted on Yard No 1366. 27.10.1981 : Launched for Lombard Leasing Services Ltd,
London, as *Bayleaf*. 20-23.3.1982 : Ran trials. 26.3.1982 : Commissioned into service, later sailing to the South
Atlantic for service during the Falklands conflict. 31.8.1982 : Returned from the South Atlantic. 1985 : Managers
became Government of the United Kingdom (Ministry of Defence, Navy Department). 1995 : Managers became
Government of The United Kingdom (The Secretary of State for Defence) (Commodore Royal Fleet Auxillary). 2001 :
Sold to the Government of the United Kingdom (Commodore RFA, managers).

The name **Hudson Sound** was allocated to this tanker but work on construction was halted at an early stage. The tanker was eventually built for bareboat charter to the Royal Fleet Auxiliary and has always sailed under the name **Bayleaf**.

(Russell Priest)

VESSELS MANAGED ON BEHALF OF DUBAI MARITIME TRANSPORT CO, PANAMA, BY JOHN HUDSON FUEL & SHIPPING LTD.

Du.1. **Jumairah**   1979

O.N.   12654g 8490n 21499d   159,01m (inc B.B.) x 22,86m x 9,67m
6-cylinder 2SA Sulzer oil engine by Astilleros Espanoles S.A. (Sestao Works), Bilbao, Spain

29.5.1976 : Launched by Union Naval de Levant S.A., Valencia, Spain, (Yard No 134) for Dubai Maritime Transport Co, Panama, (Harrisons [London] Ltd, London, managers), as **Jumairah**. 11.1976 : Completed. 1979 : Managers became John Hudson Fuel & Shipping Ltd, London. 1979 : Sold to Evdomon Corporation, Piraeus, (Gourdomichalis Maritime SA, Piraeus, managers) and renamed **Kavo Peiratis**. 1995 : Sold to Herakles Shipping Co Ltd, Bangkok, (Thoresen & Co [Bangkok] Ltd, Bangkok, managers), and renamed **Herakles**.

Jumairah on charter to Suma Line carries a full cargo of packaged timber.

(Author's collection)

Du.2. **Mishref**   1979

O.N.   12654g 8490n 21500d   159,01m (inc B.B.) x 22,84m x 9,765m
6-cylinder 2SA Sulzer oil engine by Astilleros Espanoles S.A. (Manises Works), Valencia, Spain

11.12.1976 : Launched by Union Naval de Levant S.A., Valencia, Spain, (Yard No 135) for Dubai Maritime Transport Co, Dubai, (Harrisons [London] Ltd, London, managers) as **Mishref** (Panama flag). 5.1977 : Completed. 1979 : Managers became John Hudson Fuel & Shipping Ltd, London. 1979 : Sold to Ekton Corporation, Piraeus (Gourdomichalis Maritime S.A., Piraeus, managers) and renamed **Kavo Matapas**. 1988 : Sold to Plaxtol Shipping Co Ltd, (John J Rigos Marine Enterprises S.A., Piraeus, managers), and renamed **Ioannis R** (Cyprus flag). 1995 : Sold to unidentified Panama flag owners and renamed **Hero II**. 1995 : Sold to Hero Shipping Co Ltd, Bangkok, (Thoresen & Co [Bangkok] Ltd, Bangkok, managers), and renamed **Hero**. 2001 : Sold to Kamdar Associate, India, for demolition. 2.11.2001 : beached at Alang.

Mishref

(O H Cook)

VESSELS WHOSE TECHNICAL MANAGEMENT WAS CARRIED OUT BY JOHN HUDSON FUEL AND SHIPPING LTD, ON BEHALF OF DUBAI MARITIME TRANSPORT CO, DUBAI, UNITED ARAB EMIRATES

Du.3. **Gazala**   1979
O.N.   470g 329n 439d   66,38m x 8,54m x 3,048m

2 x 6-cylinder 2SA Alpha oil engines, each driving two screws by A/S Burmeister & Wain, Maskin og Skibbyggeri, Copenhagen, Denmark.

30.10.1963 : Launched by Soc Anon des Ancien Chantiers Dubigeon, Nantes-Chantenay, France, (Yard No 806) for Gazocean SA, Paris, later Gazocean Armement, Paris, as **Monge**. 2.1964 : Completed. 1969 : Sold to Bishop Marine Inc, Dublin, and renamed **Alyce Bishop** (Panama flag). 1973 : Sold to Cia de Nav Sincero SA, Panama and renamed **Sincerogas**. 1974 : Sold to Shaikh Rashid Bin Said Al Maktoum, Dubai, United Arab Emirates, and renamed **Gazala**. 1985 : Sold to Mubarak Shipping Co, Dubai; renamed **Al Gazala**. 1985 : Sold to Pakistani shipbreakers and broken up at Gadani Beach.

Du.4. **Karama**   1979

O.N. UAE/D/646   500g 338n 640d   60,20m x 10,24m x 3,353m
6-cylinder 4 SA oil engine by Motorenwerke Mannheim AG, Mannheim, West Germany.

2.7.1965 : Launched by Falkenbergs Varv. AB, Falkenberg, Sweden, (Yard No 142) for Rederi A/B Nordic, Sweden, (F H Andersson, Stockholm, managers), as **Fahrenheit**. 10.1965 : Completed. 1971 : Managers became Ake Wanander, later Wanander Rederierna, Stockholm. 1976 : Sold to Shaikh Rashid Bin Said Al Maktoum, Dubai, United Arab Emirates, and renamed **Karama**. 1988 : Converted to an oil bunkering tanker. 1999 : Sold to Hussain A Kadhim, Dubai, and renamed **Tyba** (Belize flag). 2001 : Sold to San Diego Investments Corp, Dubai, renamed **Al Burgahm** and transferred to the Panamanian register.

The **Karama** undergoing survey and refit at Dubai Drydocks. The heavy tyre fenders indicate her use as a bunkering tanker.

(Dubai Maritime)

Du.5 *Baraha*   1979

O.N. UAE/D/647   263g 154n 345d   36,71m x 10,19m x 1,84m
6-cylinder 4SA oil engine by Caterpillar Tractor Co, Peoria, United States of America.

1.1976 : Completed by Asia-Pacific Shipyard (Pte) Ltd, Singapore, (Yard No 176) for Shaikh Rashid Bin Said Al Maktoum, Dubai, United Arab Emirates, as *Baraha*. 1998 : Sold to Al-Jazeera Shipping Co, W.L.L., Bahrain. 2001 : sold to Al Zayer Marine Services, Bahrain.

VESSELS MANAGED ON BEHALF OF TOWNSEND CAR FERRIES LTD, DOVER, BY HUDSON STEAMSHIP CO LTD

TC1. *Varangfjell*   1973 - 1979

O.N. 7333236   64741g 44000n 116,092d   866' 6" (inc BB) x 134' 0" x 52'1$\frac{1}{2}$"
9-cylinder 2SA   B & W oil engine by Uddevallavarvet A/B, Uddevalla, Sweden

27.9.1973 : Launched by Uddevallavarvet A/B, Uddevalla, Sweden, (Yard No 249) for Townsend Car Ferries Ltd, Dover, (Hudson Steamship Co Ltd, London, managers) as *Varangfjell*. 12.1973 : Completed. 1979 : Sold to Transportacion Maritima SA, Mexico. 1979 : Sold to Ore Oil Carriers Inc, New York, renamed *Enterprise* and transferred to Liberian register. 1981 : Managers became Souter Shipping Ltd, Newcastle upon Tyne. 1982 : Transferred to Panamanian register. 1983 : Sold to Enterprise Shipping Co Ltd, Bermuda (Souter Shipping Ltd, Newcastle upon Tyne, managers) and transferred to Hong Kong Register. 1996 : Sold to Pakistani shipbreakers. 12.6.1996 : arrived for demolition at Gadani Beach.

*A splendid view of the bulk carrier **Varangfjell** taken from an official company postcard.*

(Courtesy Captain D Wiley)

VESSELS MANAGED ON BEHALF OF THORNHOPE SHIPPING CO LTD
BY HUDSON STEAMSHIP CO LTD

Th.1 **Garrison Point** / **Elizabete** (2)   1977 - 1989

O.N. 377156   8014g 3980n 12330d   128,02m x 19,56m x 8,116m
12-cylinder 4SA Pielstick Vee oil engine, single reduction geared to screw shaft by Crossley Premier Engines Ltd, Manchester

5.8.1976 : Launched by Robb Caledon Shipbuilders Ltd, Leith, (Yard No 520) for Thornhope Shipping Co Ltd, London, (Hudson Steamship Co Ltd, Brighton, managers) as **Garrison Point**. 1.1977 : Completed. 1984 : Owners became Thornhope Ltd (Hudson Steamship Co Ltd, Brighton, managers). 1987 : Owners became Thornhope Shipping Co Ltd (Hudson Steamship Co Ltd, Brighton, managers). 1987 : Renamed **Elizabete** and transferred to the Bahamas register. 1989 : Sold to Joint Lease Ltd, (Stephenson Clarke Shipping Ltd, Newcastle upon Tyne, managers) and renamed **Jevington**, with Bahamas registry retained. 1992 : Transferred to the UK register. 1997 : Transferred to the Isle of Man register. 2000 : Sold to Spanish shipbreakers after being declared a constructive total loss following damage to her main engine. 27.4.2000 : Arrived at Santander in tow of the tug **Towing Diamond** from Le Havre.

The **Garrison Point** was photographed as she headed down the Thames past Gravesend in the lower photograph, whilst the view on the right shows the same vessel when trading as **Elizabete**.

(J K Byass, lower, and G Atkinson, right)

Th.2 **Warden Point**   1980 - 1990

O.N. 388629   3895g 2377n 6440d   105,64m x 14,94m x 6,839m
12-cylinder 4SA Vee oil engine, single reduction geared to a screw shaft by Alpha Diesels A/S Frederikshavn, Denmark

23.11.1977 : Launched by Götaverken Solvesborg A/B, Solvesborg, Sweden, (Yard No 87) for MS Red Sea, Sweden, (Allan Lundqvist, Kalmar, managers) as **Red Sea**. 3.1978 : Completed. 1980 : Sold to Finance for Shipping Ltd, later Investors in Industry Plc, later 3i Plc, disponent owners The Thornhope Shipping Co Ltd, (Hudson Steamship Co Ltd, Brighton, managers) and renamed **Warden Point**. 2.1990 : Sold to The Queensland Cement & Lime Co Ltd, Darra, Queensland, Australia, (Hudson Steamship Co Ltd, Brighton, managers), and transferred to the Bahamas register for her Europe - Australia delivery voyage. Converted en route at Singapore to a self-discharging cement carrier. 4.1990 : Managers became Cementco Shipping Pty Ltd, Ormiston, Queensland, and transferred to Australian register. 2003 : sold to A & B Shipping SA (Shinho Maritime Co Ltd, Pusan, South Korea, managers), and renamed **J Young** (Panama flag).

Warden Point lies at buoys on the River Tyne as she awaits her next cargo on 17 April 1988.

(Roy Cressey)

Th.3 *Crusader Point* 1980 - 1987

O.N. 390725 5972g 3631n 7300d 121,82m x 17,63m x 8,827m
  After 1987 6684g 2005n 7805d 130,00m x 17,81m x 7,570m
6-Cylinder 2SA MAN oil engine by VEB Maschinenbau Halberstadt, Halberstadt, German Democratic Republic.

3.1980 : Completed by VEB Schiffwerft "Neptun", Rostock, German Democratic Republic (Yard No 489) for Shangri La Shipping (Pte) Ltd, Singapore, as *Beate*. 1980 : Sold to Equipment Leasing Co Ltd, disponent owners The Thornhope Shipping Co Ltd, (Hudson Steamship Co Ltd, Brighton, managers) and renamed *Crusader Point*. 27.6.86 : Laid up at Hartlepool. 1987 : Sold to m.t. "Olefine Gas" GmbH & Co. Gas Carrier KG (Helmut Bastian Reederei, Bremen, managers), West Germany, and renamed *Olefine Gas*. Lengthened and converted at Hamburg to a liquefied gas tanker. 1989 : Managers became Hartmann Schiffahrts GmbH & Co KG, Leer, West Germany. 1990 : Owners became "Chem Olefine" Gas Tanker Shipping GmbH, West Germany, (Helmut Bastian Reedererei, Bremen, managers), and renamed *Chem Olefine*. 1991 : Renamed *Norgas Traveller*. 1995 : Transferred to the Liberian register. 1999 : Sold to Norwegian Gas Carriers Ltd (V Ships Norway A/S, Oslo, managers), Norway. 2000 : Managers became Norwegian Gas Carriers AS, Oslo. 2001 : Owners became Norgas Ltd, (Norwegian Gas Carriers AS, Oslo, managers). 2003 : Managers became Norgas Carriers AS, Oslo.

The *Crusader Point* is seen fully laden in the New Waterway. Her funnel bears the Thornhope markings and this view depicts her final appearance in the company fleet when all cargo handling gear had been removed. Her appearance was to be changed more radically in the late 1980s when she was lengthened and converted to a liquefied gas tanker.

(J K Byass)

Th.4 **Sir Alexander Glen**   1983 - 1989

O.N. 363587   91178g 67937n 169,044d   294,19m x 44,28m x 18,441m
8-cylinder 2SA Burmeister & Wain oil engine by Harland & Wolff Ltd, Belfast

14.11.1974 : Launched by Swan Hunter Shipbuilders Ltd, Haverton Hill on Tees, (Yard No 55) for Thornhope Shipping Co Ltd (Houlder Bros & Co Ltd, London, managers) as **Sir Alexander Glen**. 4.1975 : Completed. 1977 : Managers became Denholm Ship Management Ltd, Glasgow. 1983 : Managers became Hudson Steamship Co Ltd, Brighton. 1984 : Owners became Thornhope Ltd (Hudson Steamship Co Ltd, Brighton, managers). 1985 : Transferred to the Hong Kong register. 1987 : Owners became Thornhope Shipping Co Ltd (Hudson Steamship Co Ltd, Brighton, managers). 1988 : Transferred to the Bahamas register. 1989 : Sold to Renova Navigation Co Ltd, Cyprus, and renamed **Sir Alexander**, although she did not trade under this name. 1989 : Managers became Ji Sheng Marine Corp, Taipei, Taiwan, and renamed **Ocean Monarch**. 1989 : Sold to Edi Marine Carriers Ltd, Taipei. 1989 : Renamed **Ocean Mandarin**. 19.3.1994 : While on a voyage from Vancouver to South Korea with a cargo of coal, she lost her rudder in a position 46.45N,158.41E and

*When working in the Seateam pool, the **Sir Alexander Glen** called only once at a UK port when she discharged a part cargo of iron ore at Port Talbot in 1983. It is not surprising, therefore, that few photographs of her are available. However, this is a fine view of her underway in ballast in open sea.*
(Author's collection)

arrived in tow of **Salvage Giant** and **Salvage Queen**. 30.4.1994 : arrived at Samchonpo, South Korea. 18.5.1994 : Berthed at Kepco Pier, Samchonpo, to discharge her cargo which was completed on 27.5.1994. The vessel was then moved to the anchorage following her arrest by lawyers acting on behalf of the salvage tugs' owners. 1995 : Sold to Chinese shipbreakers. 18.10.1995 : Sailed Samchonpo bound for Xinhui for demolition.

Th.5 **Coral**   1986 - 1991

O.N. 399868   1599g 910n 4030d   86,52m (inc BB) x 14,36m x 6,763m
6-cylinder 4SA Deutz oil engine by Hijos de J Barreras, Vigo, Spain.

9.6.1979 : Launched by Sociedad Metalurgica Duro Felguera S.A., Gijon, Spain, (Yard No 147) for its own account as **Duro Seis**. 8.1979 : Completed. 1982 : Renamed **Puerto De Aguilas**. 1983 : Managers became Sociedad Naviera Box Marine S.A., Madrid, Spain, and renamed **Coral**. 1985 : Acquired by Senior Navigation Ltd, Liberia, (Hudson Steamship Co Ltd, Brighton, managers) and transferred to Bahamas register. 1986 : Owners became Thornhope Shipping Co Ltd (Hudson Steamship Co Ltd, Brighton, managers) with Bahamas registry retained. 1991 : Sold to Jomfruland Transport NV, (Sandfirden Rederij BV, Groningen, managers), and renamed **Coral Sea** (Netherlands Antilles flag). 1994 : Managers became Jarin Technical Services BV. 1995 : Managers became Rialto Shipping BV, Farsum, Holland. 1995 : Sold to Coral Sea Shipping Ltd, (Brise Schiffahrts GmbH, Leer, managers); converted to a cement carrier at Dordrecht by Merewido BV; on completion,

Coral

(Company archives)

renamed **Cemsea** (Antigua & Barbuda flag). 7.2003 : sold to Pan Nautic S A., Lugano, Switzerland; transferred to the Panamanian register and renamed **Cemash**. 8.2003 : Owners became Coral Sea Shipping Ltd, (Brise Schiffahrts, managers); transferred to the Antigua & Barbuda register and renamed **Cemsea**. 9.2003 : sold to United Marine SA (Nafto Trade Shipping & Commercial SA, Piraeus, managers). Renamed **Nafto Cement VI** (St Vincent & the Grenadines flag).

Th.6 *Mosstar* 1988 - 1991

O.N. N-00299 10287g 7104n 16016d 141,51m (inc. BB) x 22,3m x 9,391m
2SA B & W oil engine by Hitachi Zosen, Sakurajima, Japan.

7.3.1978 : Launched by Kanda Zosensho KK, Kawajiri, Japan, (Yard No 229) for Panama Transworld Leasing SA Panama (Ahijin Shipping Co Ltd, Seoul, South Korea, managers) as *Africanstars*. 5.1978 : Completed. 1981 : Managers became J R Teihcson & Management Co Ltd, Hong Kong. 1986 : Sold to Mistral Navigation Co, Cyprus, (Arapko Compania Naviera SA, Piraeus, managers) and renamed *Arko Star*. 1988 : Acquired by Thornhope Shipping Co Ltd (Hudson Steamship Co Ltd, Brighton, managers), renamed *Mosstar* and transferred to the Bahamas register. 1991 : Sold to Dalarik Shipping Co Ltd, Cyprus, (Hudson Steamship Co Ltd, Brighton, managers). 1992 : Managers became Ormos Compania Naviera SA, Piraeus, and renamed *Cosstar*. 1994 : Renamed *Conor*. 1997 : Sold to Caruso Shipping Corp, (Moss Marine Management S.A., managers) and renamed *Chian Trader* (Liberia flag). 1998 : Managers became Levant Maritime International SA, Piraeus. 2001 : Sold to Pigassos SA, Liberia, (Seabirds Maritime SA, Piraeus, managers) and renamed *Pigassos*. 2003 : Sold to Indian breakers. 7.3.2003 : Beached at Alang for demolition.

Mosstar

(Dag Bakka jr)

Th.7 *Mosdeep* 1989 - 1996

O.N. 715358 30017g 18012n 49000d 190,02m (inc BB) x 32,24m x 12,118m
8-cylinder 2SA Mitsubishi oil engine by Ube Industries Ltd, Ube, Japan.

7.8.1981 : Launched by Kasado Dockyard Co Ltd, Kudomatsu, Japan, (Yard No 326) for Yamashita-Shinnihon Kisen KK and Sanwa Shosen KK, Tokyo, Japan, as *Yamaoki Maru*. 11.1981 : Completed. 1986 : Managers became Yamashita-Shinnihon Kisen KK, Tokyo. 1988 : Sold to Dan Merchant Ltd, Bahamas, (A/S Det Ostasiatiske Kompagnie, Copenhagen, managers), and renamed *Casuarina*. 1989 : Owners became Casu Transport Ltd, Bahamas, (A/S Det Ostasiatiske Kompagnie, Copenhagen, managers). 1989 : Acquired by Thornhope Shipping Co Ltd, (Hudson Steamship Co Ltd, Brighton, managers), and renamed *Mosdeep* with Bahamas registry retained. 1996 : Managers became Mosvold Shipping AS, Kristiansand. 1998 : Sold to Sunrunner Navigation Corp, (Byzantine Marine Corp, Piraeus, managers), and renamed *Fanoula* (Bahamas flag). 2003 : sold to Seaborn Maritime Co (Hellenic American Shipmanagement Inc, Athens, managers). Renamed *Fanfare* (Panama flag).

Mosdeep

(Author's collection)

The **Mosdeep** under her original name of **Yamaoki Maru**.

(J Y Freeman)

Th.8 **Mos Freeway** 1989 - 1990

O.N. 715447 2841g 1513n 5273d 122,81m (inc BB) x 18,36m x 6,201m
2 x 8-cylinder 4SA MAN oil engines by Empresa Nacional 'Bazan' de CNM SA, Cartagena, Spain.

22.12.1980 : Launched by Enrique Lorenzo y Cia. SA, Vigo, Spain (Yard No 400) for Internacional Roll-On Roll-Off SA (INTERROLL), Spain, as **Roll Vigo**. 12.1981 : Completed. 1985 : Sold to Interpuertos SA, Spain. 1985 : Renamed **Burgos**. 1989 : Sold to Lux Freeway Shipping, (Colonial Marine Industries Inc, Savannah, managers) and renamed **Lux Freeway** (Vanuatu flag). 1989 : Sold to Bos Freeway Shipping Ltd, (Acomarit Services Maritimes SA, Geneva, managers) and renamed **Bos Freeway** (Bahamas flag). 1989 : Acquired by Thornhope Shipping Co Ltd (Hudson Steamship Co Ltd, Brighton, managers), renamed **Mos Freeway** with Bahamas registry retained. 1990 : Sold to Compania Transmediterranea SA, Madrid, and renamed **Ciudad de Burgos** (Spain flag).

The **Mos Freeway** under her original identity of **Roll Vigo**.

(Author's collection)

Th.9 **Moscliff** 1993 - 1995

O.N. 711132 126,943g 96943n 256,712d 348,72m (inc BB) x 51,87m x 20,046m
After 2002 120,545g 86952n 256,033d
2 x General Electric Steam Turbines, double reduction geared to a single shaft by A G Weser, Bremen, West Germany.

26.3.1974 : Launched by A G Weser, Bremen, West Germany, (Yard No 1378) for Esso Tankvaart Nederlandse Antillen NV (Esso Tankvaart Maatschappij BV, Rotterdam, managers), Netherlands Antilles, as **Esso Saba**. 7.1974 : Completed. 1980 : Managers become Esso Tankvaart Maatschappij BV, Rotterdam. 10.10.1983 : Arrived in Brunei Bay, Sabah, for lay-up. 1987 : Owners became Esso International Shipping (Bahamas) Co Ltd, Bahamas; renamed **Esso Freeport** and returned to service from lay-up. 6.11.1987 : Suffered minor damage after being attacked by Iranian gunboats in a position 25.47N, 55.24E while on passage from Ras Tanura to USA. 1993 : Sold to Thornhope Shipping Co Ltd, (Hudson Steamship Co Ltd, Brighton, managers) and renamed **Moscliff** with Bahamas registry retained. 1995 : Managers became Mosvold Shipping AS, Kristiansand. 1998 : Owners became Moscliff Investment Ltd (Mosvold Shipping AS, Kristiansand, managers), Bahamas. 2002 : Sold to SBM Services Inc (Single Buoy Moorings Inc, Marly, Switzerland, managers). Converted to a floating production, storage, offtake vessel. Renamed **FPSO Brasil**.

Moscliff

(M Lennon, Dag Bakka jr collection)

VESSELS MANAGED ON BEHALF OF CARLESS SOLVENTS LTD, LONDON, BY HUDSON STEAMSHIP CO LTD

Ca.1 **Carsol**   1979 - 1982   Motor Tanker
O.N. 388262   500g 320n 1050d   206' 11" x 31' 7" x 12' 4"
6-cylinder 2SA oil engine by Alpha Diesel A/S Frederikshavn, Denmark

25.6.1964 : Launched by Fr. Lürssen Werft GmbH, Bremen-Vegesack, West Germany, (Yard No 13359) for Rederei I/S Coastaltanker, Århus, (Neils B Terkildsen, Århus, managers) as **Lisbet Terkol**. 7.1964 : Completed. 1972 : Managers became Terkildsen & Olsen A/S, Århus. 1973 : Owners became R/I Coastaltanker, Århus, (Terkildsen & Olsen A/S, Århus, managers). 1982 : Acquired by Carless Solvents Ltd, London, (Hudson Steamship Co Ltd, Brighton, managers) and renamed **Carsol**. 1982 : Sold to G N Sanakis Towing, Piraeus, and renamed **Agios Symeon**. 1987 : Sold to Nearchos Maritime Co, Athens, and renamed **Mytilini**. 1992 : Sold to Anoymous Elliniki Eteria Petreleoidon G Mamidakis & Co, Piraeus. 1995 : Sold to Nearchos Maritime Co, Piraeus.

Carsol passing beneath the Forth Bridge.

(Jim Prentice)

Ca.2 *Landguard Point*   1982 - 1986

O.N. 398948   4968g 2779n 8161d   108,46m x 18,24m x 7,379m
    After 1992   5323g 1597n 6706d
6-cylinder 2SA Mitsubishi oil engine by Akasaka Tekkosho KK (Akasaka Diesels Ltd), Yaizu, Japan

7.10.1981 : Launched by Miho Zosensko KK, Shimizu, (Yard No 1181) for Carless Solvents Ltd, London, (Hudson Steamship Co Ltd, Brighton, managers) as *Landguard Point*. 1.1982 : Completed. 1986 : Sold to Carib Carriers Ltd, (Colonial Navigation Inc, Savannah, Georgia, managers) and renamed *Mrs B* (Bahamas flag). 1987 : Sold to S.P. Shipping Co Ltd, (Slobodna Plovidba, Sibenik, managers) and renamed *Beograd* (Yugoslavia flag). 1988 : Sold to Splosna Plovba Piran, Potorz, Yugoslavia. 1988 : Sold to Abbotswood Shipping Corp, (Monrovia Slobodna Plovidba, Sibenik, managers). 1991 : Sold to Waterbury Shipping Co Ltd, Panama. 1991 : Sold to Koppers Shipping Pty (BHP Transport, later BHP Transport & Logistics Pty Ltd, Melbourne, Victoria, managers), Australia. 1991/92 : Converted at Singapore to a hot cargo chemical tanker and renamed *Seakap* (Australia flag). 2001 : Managers became Teekay Shipping (Australia) Pty Ltd, Sydney, New South Wales.

Landguard Point at the beginning of what is thought to be her delivery voyage from Japan.

         (Company archives)

VESSELS MANAGED ON BEHALF OF THE MINISTRY OF SHIPPING, LATER MINISTRY OF WAR TRANSPORT, LATER MINISTRY OF TRANSPORT

MT.1 *Elizabete* (1)   1940 - 1952

O.N. 167820   2039g 1265n   251.0' x 44.0' x 20.0'
T.3-cylinder engine made by American Shipbuilding Co, Cleveland, Ohio, USA

7.1917 : Completed by American Shipbuilding Co, Cleveland, Ohio, USA, (Yard No 466), for Atlantic Gulf West Indies Transportation Co, New York, USA, as *Kiowa*. 1919 : Owners became Atlantic Gulf & West Indies Steamship Lines, New York. 1920 : Sold to Clyde Steamship Co Inc, New York, USA. 1928 : Sold to D W Haydon, Riga, Latvia, and renamed *Valka*. 1929 : Sold to Peter Schwans & Co, Riga, Latvia, and renamed *Kurzeme*. 1934 : Sold to Mrs E Katkevics, Riga, Latvia, and renamed *Elizabete*. 1934 : Managers became A Katkevics, Riga, Latvia. 15.10.1940 : Taken over by The Ministry of Transport, later Ministry of War Transport, (Hudson Steamship Co Ltd, London, managers). Transferred to UK flag, with Cardiff as port of registry. 4.1946 : Owners became The Ministry of Transport (Hudson Steamship Co Ltd, London, managers). 1952 : Sold to Brila Shipping Co Ltd, London, (Hudson Steamship Co Ltd, London, managers). 1955 : Sold to Leo Lines Ltd, Hull, (John Carlbom & Co Ltd, Hull, managers) and renamed *Siona* with Hull as port of registry. 25.12.1957 : Laid up at Hartlepool. 1959 : Sold to British Iron and Steel Corporation for demolition. 24.11.1959 : arrived at Dunston upon Tyne having been allocated to Clayton & Davie Ltd.

Elizabete

(WSPL)

This photograph of the **Vilk** should be compared with that of her on page 15.

(W H Brown, WSPL)

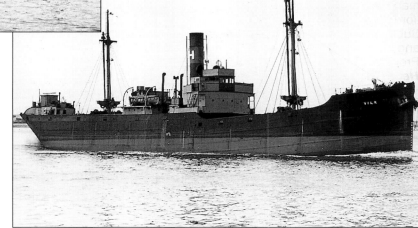

MT.2 *Vilk*   1940 - 1950

O.N. 135270   1933g 1123n   267.0' x 38.0' x 17.6'
T.3-cylinder engine by North Eastern Marine Engineering Co Ltd, Sunderland

10.1913 : Completed by S P Austin & Son Ltd, Sunderland, (Yard No 269) for W Cory & Son Ltd, London, as **Hitchin**. 1916 : Owners became Cory Colliers Ltd, London. 1920 : Renamed **Corbank**. 1939 : Sold to Tallinna Laevauhisus A/S, Estonia (Tallinn Shipping Co Ltd, Tallinn, managers) and renamed **Vilk**. 16.10.1940 : Taken over by The Ministry of Shipping, later Ministry of War Transport (Hudson Steamship Co Ltd, London, managers). Transferred to UK flag with Glasgow as port of registry. 4.1946 : Owners became The Ministry of Transport (Hudson Steamship Co Ltd, London, managers). 1950 : Sold to Cia Maritima La Villa S.A, (A/B Neuhaus & Co, Stockholm, managers) and renamed **La Villa** (Panama flag). 1957 : Sold to Van den Bossche & Co, Belgium, for demolition at their yard in Boom.

Empire Lagoon   See **Hudson Bay** No. 13 in main fleet.
Empire Pioneer   See **Hudson Bank** No. 14 in main fleet.

MT.3 *Miervaldis*   1948

O.N. 120461   1228g 758n   234.6' x 36.1' x 14.9't
T.3-cylinder engine by Clyde Shipbuilding & Engineering Co Ltd, Port Glasgow

10.1904 : Completed by Clyde Shipbuilding & Engineering Co Ltd, Port Glasgow, (Yard No 260) for Stephenson Clarke & Co, London, as **St Edmund**. 1922 : Sold to Kingsdon Steamship Co Ltd, Cardiff, and renamed **Kingsdon**. 1929 : Sold to Stahl & Co Ltd, Latvia, (D Thomsons, Riga, managers), and renamed **Miervaldis** (Latvia flag). 15.10.1940 : Taken over by The Ministry of Shipping, later Ministry of War Transport (Broomhill Steamships Ltd, Newcastle upon Tyne, managers), and registered at Swansea. 4.1946 : Owners became The Ministry of Transport (Broomhill Steamships Ltd, Newcastle upon Tyne, managers). 1948 : Managers became Hudson Steamship Co Ltd, London. 17.7.1948 : Laid up. 22.9.1948 : Scuttled in the Bay of Biscay with a cargo of 1880 tons of chemical warfare munitions.

Miervaldis

(G E Brownell, WSPL)

VESSELS MANAGED ON BEHALF OF MOSVOLD A/S, KRISTIANSAND, BY HUDSON STEAMSHIP CO LTD

Mo.1 **Mostween 2**   1988 - 1989

O.N. N-00337   9989g 6994n 16271d   147,81m (inc BB) x 21,04m x 9,259m
16-cylinder 4SA Vee oil engine by Masch. Augsburg-Nurnberg (MAN), Hamburg, West Germany

1.12.1979 : Launched by AG 'Weser' Seebeckwerft, Bremerhaven, West Germany, (Yard No. 1009), for Seafaith Bulk Carriers Corp, Liberia, (Michail A Karageorgis Lines Corp, Piraeus, managers) as **Aristogenis**. 3.1980 : Completed. 1986 : Owners became Rockfleet Bay Shipping Co Ltd, (Michail A Karageorgis SA, Piraeus, managers) and renamed **Vulcan** (Greece flag). 1988 : Acquired by Mostween 2 K/S, Kristiansand, (Hudson Steamship Co Ltd, Brighton, managers), and renamed **Mostween 2** (Norway flag). 1989 : Sold to Jordan National Shipping Lines Co Ltd, Amman, Jordan, and renamed **Jordan 1** (Jordan flag).   1994 : Sold to Hai Gwang Shipping Co Ltd, (Hebei Province Subcorporation China Ocean Shipping Co (COSCO HEBEI), Qinhuangdao, People's Republic of China, managers), and renamed **Yong Shun** (St Vincent & the Grenadines flag). 1997 : Owners became Hebei Shipping Co Ltd, (Hebei Province Subcorporation China Ocean Shipping Co (COSCO HEBEI), Qinhuangdao, managers). 2001 : Renamed **Hebei Sunlight**. 2001 : Managers became Hebei Ocean Shipping Company (COSCO HEBEI), Qinhuangdao.

Mostween 2 arriving at Antwerp.

(Dag Bakka jr)

Mo.2 **Mostank**   1988 - 1989

O.N.   60670g 45643n 123,699dwt   260,64m (inc BB) x 40,67m x 16,663m
9-cylinder 2SA Sulzer oil engine by Mitsubishi Heavy Industries Ltd, Kobe, Japan

9.6.1975 : Launched by Mitsubishi Heavy Industries Ltd, Hiroshima, Japan, (Yard No. 256) for Neptune Marine Co Ltd, Liberia, as **Galene**. 11.1975 : Completed as **Obelix** for Asterix Shipping Corp (Lindsay Blee Chartering Ltd, London, managers), having been sold while fitting out. 1979 : Sold to Statistix Shipping NV (Van Nievelt Goudriaan & Co BV, Rotterdam, managers); Liberia flag. 1982 : Sold to Trilight Tankers Ltd, (Oscar Transportation Corp Ltd, Piraeus, managers) and renamed **Trilight** (Greece flag). 1985 : Sold to Sheffield Trading Ltd, Greece, (Le Timon Transport Co, Piraeus, managers) and renamed **Elite**. 1988 : Acquired by K/S Mostank 1, Kristiansand, (Hudson Steamship Co Ltd, Brighton, managers) and renamed **Mostank** (Norway flag). 1989 : Sold to K/S Happy Elin, Norway (Billabong Ship Management A/S & Co, Oslo, managers) and renamed **Happy Elin**.   1991 : Managers became Bergen Shipmanagement A/S, Bergen and renamed **Elin**. 1991/92 : Used as a storage vessel at Widuri Terminal. 1992 : Sold to Kriti Ambassador Shipping Co SA, (Avin International Corp of Panama SA, Piraeus, managers) and renamed **Kriti Ambassador** (Greece flag). 9.11.98 : laid up at Pointe Noire. 2000 : Sold to Indian breakers. 21.1.2000 : arrived at Mumbai for demolition.

Mostank

(Dag Bakka jr)

Mo.3 *Ostfriesland*   1988 - 1990

O.N. N-00395   12974g 7348n 17800d   160,03m (inc BB) x 22,86m x 9,602m
6-cylinder 2SA oil engine by Sulzer Bros Ltd, Winterthur, Switzerland

17.10.1978 : Launched by Howaldtswerke-Deutsche Werft AG, Kiel, West Germany, (Yard No 137) for Bugsier - Reederei und Burgung AG, Hamburg, as *Ostfriesland*. 12.1978 : Completed. 1980 : Renamed *S A Ostfriesland*. 1981 : Renamed *Ostfriesland*. 1984 : Renamed *Hodeidah Crown*. 1985 : Renamed *Ostfriesland*. 1988 : Owners became Bugsier-Reederei und Bergungs GmbH, Hamburg, and transferred to the Cypriot register. 1988 : Acquired by K/S Mostween 3, Kristiansand, (Hudson Steamship Co Ltd, Brighton, managers). 1990 : Sold to Lauren Shipping Corp Pte Ltd, (Bay Ocean Management, Englewood, New Jersey, managers); Singapore flag. 1995 : Sold to Jutha Phakakrong Shipping Pte Ltd, (Bay Ocean Management Inc, Englewood, New Jersey, managers). 1996 : Renamed *Kota Selamat*. 1997 : Renamed *Ostfriesland*. 2001 : Renamed *X-Press Annapurna*. 2001 : Renamed *Ostfriesland*. 2001 : Managers became Jutha Maritime Public Co Ltd, Bangkok.

Ostfriesland

(Ron Baker)

Mo.4 **Mosbay**   1988 - 1991

O.N. N-00401   14059g 8754n 24732d   164,18m x 24,60m x 9,830m
6-cylinder 2SA Sulzer oil engine by Mitsubishi Heavy Industries Ltd, Kobe, Japan

23.7.1979 : Launched by Onomichi Zosen, Onomichi, Japan, (Yard No 281) for Richfield Navigation Co Inc, Panama, as **Van Enterprise**. 11.1979 : Completed. 1988 : Acquired by K/S Mosbulk, Kristiansand, (Hudson Steamship Co Ltd, Brighton, managers) and renamed **Mosbay**. 1991 : Sold to Torhan Uluslararasi Denizcilik ve Ticaret A.S., Turkey, and renamed **Selda**. 1994 : Sold to Kaptan Demir Celik Endustrisi ve Ticarat A.S., Istanbul, and renamed **Kaptan Cebi**. 1996 : Sold to Nidal Compania De Navegacion S A, (Jolane S.A., Lugano, managers), and renamed **Sanaga** (Panama flag). 11.10.1999 : While on a voyage from Owendo to China with a cargo of logs, she reported taking in water in No 1 hold. Down by the head 2.5 metres and at waterline level in Nos 1 and 2 holds in a position 27.34.3S, 44.13.6E, 700 miles ENE of Durban. Her 26 crew abandoned ship and were picked up by the container ship **Sagittarius Challenger**. She was then reported drifting in position 27.51.4S, 43.34.21E. 18.10.1999 : Reported sunk.

Mosbay

*(Göran Freiholtz,
Dag Bakka jr collection)*

Mo.5 **Mostween 4**   1989 - 1991

O.N. N-00489   13436g 8557n 20860d   161,60m x 22,84m x 9,932m
7-cylinder 2SA Burmeister & Wain oil engine by Hitachi Zosen, Sakurajima Works, Osaka, Japan

20.8.1975 : Launched by Hitachi Zosen, Mukaishima, Japan, (Yard No 4483) for Eridanus Maritima SA, (Overseas Maritime Ltd, Bermuda, managers) as **Jamaica Farewell** (Liberia flag). 12.1975 : Completed. 1985 : Renamed **MT Powell**. 1985 : Sold to Cheetah Shipping Co Ltd, (International Sugar Transport Inc, London, managers) and renamed **Atlantic Progress** (Cyprus flag). 1988 : Managers became Forum Maritime S.A., Piraeus, and renamed **Forum Express**. 1989 : Acquired by Mostween 4 K/S, Kristiansand, (Hudson Steamship Co Ltd, Brighton, managers) and renamed **Mostween 4** (Norway flag). 1991 : Sold to Venetico Maritime Inc. S.A., (Leond Maritime Inc, Piraeus, managers) and renamed **Angelina L** (Greece flag). 1998 : Sold to Edinburgh Maritime S.A., (OIA Maritime Co S.A., managers) and renamed **Highlander 1** (Panama flag). 2000 : Sold to Jaipur Ltd, Kingstown, St Vincent & the Grenadines, and renamed **Bombay**. 2001 : Sold to Bangladeshi shipbreakers. 12.4.2001 arrived at Chittagong for demolition.

Mostween 4

(Company archives)

Mo.6 *Mostween 5 / Napier Star / Mostween 5*   1989 - 1994

O.N. N-00540   10825g 6349n 15737d   151,24m x 21,24m x 9,468m
5-cylinder 2SA Sulzer oil engine by Mitsubishi Heavy Industries Ltd., Kobe, Japan

18.4.1977 : Launched by Mitsubishi Heavy Industries Ltd, Hiroshima, Japan, (Yard No 284) for Silverness Shipping Ltd (Silver Line Ltd, London, managers) as *Silverness*. 8.1977 : Completed. 1978 : Renamed *Taabo*. 1979 : Sold to Société Ivoirienne de Navigation Maritime, Abidjan, Ivory Coast (SIVOMAR) (Silver Line Ltd, London, managers). 1983 : Sold to Ruby Compania Naviera SA, (Mycali Maritime Corp S.A., Piraeus, managers). 1985 : Renamed *Agios Andreas* (Greece flag). 1989 : Acquired by K/S Mostween 5, Norway, (Hudson Steamship Co Ltd, Brighton, managers) and renamed *Mostween 5*. 1993 : Renamed *Napier Star*. 1994 : Renamed *Mostween 5*. 1994 : Sold to Rallia Shipping Co Ltd, (Geostral Marine S.A., Piraeus, managers, later agents only), and renamed *Rallia* (Cyprus flag). 30.1.1999 : Fire broke out in her engine room when off the coast of Crete while she was on a voyage from Zeebrugge to Iran with a cargo of bagged sugar. Most of her crew were evacuated and the fire was extinguished. She was taken in tow by the salvage tug *Agios Dimitrios* for Suda Bay. 15.9.2000 : Laid up off Kynossoura having been reported to be under arrest since April 1999 with only minimum repairs having been carried out since the engine room fire.

Mostween 5, with immaculate paintwork, suggesting that she was fresh from drydock when the photograph was taken.

(Company archives)

A very rare view of the *Mostween 5* when she was on charter to Blue Star Line in whose colours she traded as *Napier Star* for a short time.

(Russell Priest)

Mo.7 *Mostween 6 / Hyacinth Trader / Mostween 6*   1989 - 1991

O.N. N-00585   10021g 6450n 16543d   147,35m (inc BB) x 21,85m x 9,138m
6-cylinder 2SA Sulzer oil engine by Ishikawajima Harima Heavy Industries, Aioi, Japan

12.3.1977 : Launched by Hashihama Zosen, Tadotsu, Japan, (Yard No 642) for Adam Shipping Enterprises Corp, (Tredan Shipping Corp Ltd, Hong Kong, managers) as *SCT Vincent* (Liberia flag). 4.1977 : Completed. 1979 : Renamed *Sainte Suzanne*. 1982 : Managers became A P Madgrigal Steamship Co Inc, Manila. 1984 : Managers became Amas Navigation Co Ltd, Hong Kong. 1986 : Sold to Helmut Hermann Shipping Co Ltd, (Josef Roth Reederei, Hamburg, managers) and renamed *Bavaria Star* (Cyprus flag). 1988 : Owners became Bavaria Star Maritime Co Ltd, Cyprus, (KG Reederei Roth GmbH, Hamburg, managers). 1989 : Acquired by K/S Mostween 6, Kristiansand, (Hudson Steamship Co Ltd, Brighton, managers); renamed *Mostween 6*. 1990 : Renamed *Hyacinth Trader*. 1990 : Renamed *Mostween 6*. 1991 : Sold to Ming Sung Carrier Panama S A, (Ming Sung Shipping Co [Hong Kong] Ltd, Hong Kong, managers) and renamed *Lung Meng* (Panama flag). 1999 : Sold to Chuang He Shipping Ltd (Zhong Shan Shipping Co Ltd, Hong Kong, managers), and renamed *Chuang Ye (*St Vincent & the Grenadines flag).

Mostween 6

(M Lennon, Dag Bakka jr collection)

Mo.8 **Mostween 8**   1989 - 1992

O.N. N-00600   13911g 7162n 20412d   153,50m (inc BB) x 22,76m x 10,081m
5-cylinder 2SA Burmeister & Wain oil engine by Mitsui Engineering & Shipbuilding Co Ltd, Tamano, Japan

20.02.1984 : Launched by Hayashikane Shipbuilding & Engineering Co Ltd, Shimonoseki, Japan, (Yard No 1277) for Silver Gulf Shipping Co. SA, (Stavros Daifas Marine Enterprises S.A., Piraeus, managers) as **Silver Gulf** (Greece flag). 5.1984 : Completed. 1989 : Acquired by Mostween 8 K/S, Kristiansand, (Hudson Steamship Co Ltd, managers), and renamed **Mostween 8** (Norway flag). 1992 : Sold to Pascal International Inc (Sudamericana Scheepvaartmaatschappij BV, Rotterdam, managers), and renamed **Ushuaia** (Liberia flag). 1994 : Sold to Attica Shipping Co Ltd, (Dockendale Shipping Co Ltd, Nassau, managers). 1995 : Renamed **Attica** (Bahamas flag). 1996 : Renamed **Vaimama**. 1997 : Renamed **Attica**. 1999 : Renamed **Albert Oldendorff**. 2000 : Renamed **DS Attica**. 2004 : Renamed **African Sanderling**.

Mostween 8

(Torsten Andreas)

Mo.9 *Mostween 7*   1989 - 1995

O.N. N-00618   10555g 7372n 16363d   148,52m (inc BB) x 21,81m x 9,138m
5-Cylinder 2SA Sulzer oil engine by Ishikawajima-Harima Heavy Industries, Aio, Japan

25.5.1977: Launched by Hashihama Zosen, Tadotsu, Japan, (Yard No 639) for Pressos Compania Naviera S.A., (G & N Angelakis Shipping Co S A, Piraeus, managers), as *Nicholaos Angelakis*. 9.1977 : Completed. 1978 : Sold to Helmut Hermann Shipping Co Ltd, (Josef Roth Reederei, Hamburg, managers) and renamed *Helmut Hermann* (Cyprus flag). 1989 : Managers became Uniteam Marine Ltd, Limassol. 1989 : Acquired by Mostween 7 K/S, Kristiansand, (Hudson Steamship Co Ltd, Brighton, managers) and renamed *Mostween 7* (Norway flag). 1995 : Sold to Rhonda Maritime Corp, (Acomarit-LPL [Hellas], Piraeus, managers), and renamed *Mattheos L* (St Vincent & the Grenadines flag). 2002 : Managers became V-Ships Greece Ltd, Piraeus. 2002 : Sold to Saumil Impex Pvt. Ltd, India, for demolition. 21.8. 2002 beached at Alang.

The *Mostween 7* discharges a cargo of sugar at Tate & Lyle's Thames Refinery Jetty on 5 February 1992.

(Tony Hogwood)

Mo.10 *Mosgulf*   1989 - 1992

O.N. N-00662   20791g 11539n 33329d   196,32m (inc BB) x 25,86m x 10,956m
10-cylinder 2SA MAN Vee oil engine by Maschinenbau Augsburg, Augsburg, West Germany

2.9.1971 : Launched by Lübecker Flender-Werke AG, Lübeck, West Germany, (Yard No 590) for Lübeck Linie AG, West Germany, as *Possehl*. 12.1971 : Completed. 1981 : Sold to Indubio Maritime Inc, (Diana Shipping Agencies, Piraeus, managers), and renamed *Zetta* (Greece flag). 1987 : Owners became Summer Star Shipping, (Diana Shipping Services, Piraeus, managers); transferred to Cyprus flag. 1989 : Acquired by Mosbulk III K/S, Kristiansand, (Hudson Steamship Co Ltd, Brighton, managers), and renamed *Mosgulf* (Norway flag). 1992 : Sold to Sealion Shipping (St Vincent) Ltd, (Jiangsu Marine Shipping Co, Nanjing/Nanking, People's Republic of China, managers), and renamed *Welda* (St. Vincent and the Grenadines flag). 2000 : Managers became Shenzhen Daxi Marine Shipping Co Ltd, Shenzhen, People's Republic of China.

Mosgulf

(Author's collection)

Mo.11 **Mosriver** 1989 - 1994

O.N. N-00727   19650g 14305n 35555d   185,50m (inc BB) x 26,04m x 11,148m
7-cylinder 2SA Sulzer oil engine by Mitsubishi Heavy Industries Ltd, Kobe, Japan

2.4.1972 : Launched by Osaka Zosensho, Osaka, Japan, (Yard No 327) for Maxim Shipping Co Inc, (International Maritime Carriers Ltd, Hong Kong, managers) as **Maritime Fortune** (Panama flag). 7.1972 : Completed. 1982 : Sold to Arabian Maritime Transport Co Ltd (AMTC), Jeddah, Saudi Arabia, and renamed **Saqr Yanbu**. 1987 : Managers became Al Sabah Maritime Services Co Ltd, Jeddah. 1987 : Sold to Goodray Shipping Co Ltd, Limassol, and renamed **Bolero**. 1987 : Managers became Styga Compania Naviera S.A., Piraeus, and renamed **Candia**. 1988 : Sold to Oceanage Shipping Ltd, (Styga Compania Naviera S.A., Piraeus, managers). 1989 : Acquired by Mosbulk 5 K/S, Kristiansand, (Hudson Steamship Co Ltd, Brighton, managers) and renamed **Mosriver** (Norway flag). 1994 : Sold to Great Eastern Shipping Co London Ltd, London, (The Great

Mosriver

(van Ginderen collection, WSPL)

Eastern Shipping Co Ltd, Bombay, managers), and renamed **Anuradha** (Bahamas flag). 1998 : Sold to Bangladeshi shipbreakers. About 15.5.1998 arrived at Chittagong for demolition.

Mo.12 **Moslake** 1989 - 1993

O.N. N-00786   20045g 14825n 34749d   194,52m (inc BB) x 27,18m x 10,653m
7-cylinder 2SA Sulzer oil engine by G Clark & NEM Ltd, Wallsend.

28.1.1971 : Launched by Doxford & Sunderland Ltd, Deptford Shipyard, Sunderland, (Yard No 847) for Ancla Maritime S.A. Piraeus, (Lyras Bros Ltd., London), as **John Lyras**. 7.1971 : Completed. 1986 : Sold to Almea Maritime Co Ltd, (Link Line Ltd, Piraeus, managers), and renamed **Althea** (Cyprus flag). 1989 : Acquired by Mosbulk 4 K/S, Kristiansand, (Hudson Steamship Co Ltd, Brighton, managers), and renamed **Moslake** (Norway flag). 1993 : Sold to Seaeagle Shipping Ltd, , (Jiangsu Marine Shipping Co, Nanjing, People's Republic of China, managers), and renamed **Xingda** (St. Vincent and the Grenadines flag). 1993 : Managers became Shenzhen Daxi Marine Shipping Co Ltd., Shenzen, People's Republic of China. 1996 : Owners became Xin Venus Shipping Co Ltd, Shenzen, People's Republic of China. 1998 : Sold to Indian shipbreakers. 25.7.1998 : Arrived at Alang for demolition.

Moslake

(Author's collection)

*Two vessels named **Moslake** have given rise to confusion. To confirm that the vessel above is indeed that managed by Hudson Steamship, we see her under her original name of **John Lyras**.*

(WSPL)

Mo.13 **Mosdale** 1991 - 1992

O.N. N-01136   35350g 21475n 66041d   225,00m (inc BB) x 32,24m x 12,901m
6-cylinder 2SA B&W oil engine by Hyundai Engine & Machinery Co Ltd, Ulsan, South Korea

16.12.1989 : Launched by Daewoo Shipbuilding & Heavy Machinery Ltd, Okpo, Koje, South Korea, (Yard No 1050) for Czechoslovak Ocean Shipping International Joint Stock Co (Ceskoslovenska Namorni Plavba), Czechoslavakia, as **Sumnava 5**. 1990 : Completed and laid up by the builders after her owners refused delivery. 10.1991 : Acquired by Mosvold Shipping AS, Kristiansand, (Hudson Steamship Co Ltd, Brighton, managers), and renamed **Mosdale**. 1992 : Sold to Ilex Shipping Co Ltd, (Qingdao Ocean Shipping Company (COSCO QINGDAO), Qingdao/Tsingtao, People's Republic of China, managers), and renamed **Sea Ilex** (Malta flag). 1993 : Managers became Tat On Shipping & Enterprises Co Ltd. 1995 : Managers became Qingdao Ocean Shipping Company (COSCO QINGDAO) Qingdao/Tsingtao, People's Republic of China. 2001 : Managers became Cosbulk Carrier Co Ltd (COSBULK), Tianjin, People's Republic of China. Transferred to Panama flag.

A busy scene at the builder's yard in South Korea as the **Mosdale** is assisted by tugs possibly at the start of a trials or a delivery voyage.

(Company archives)

Mo.14 **Moshill** 1991 - 1992

O.N. N-01137   35350g 21472n 66043d   225,00m (inc BB) x 32,24m x 12,900m
6-cylinder 2SA B & W oil engine by Hyundai Engine & Machinery Co Ltd, Ulsan, South Korea

28.4.1990 : Launched by Daewoo Shipbuilding and Heavy Machinery Ltd, Okpo, Koje, South Korea, (Yard No. 1051) for Czechoslovak Ocean Shipping International Joint Stock Co (Ceskoslovenska Namorni Plavba), Prague, Czechoslavkia, as **Beskydy**. 8.1990 : Completed and laid up by the builders after her owners refused delivery. 10.1991 : Acquired by Mosvold Shipping AS, Kristiansand, (Hudson Steamship Co. Ltd, Brighton, managers), and renamed **Moshill**. 1992 : Sold to Magnolia Shipping Co Ltd (Qingdao Ocean Shipping Company [COSCO QINGDAO]), Qingdao/Tsingtao, People's Republic of China, managers), and renamed **Sea Magnolia** (Malta flag). 1993 : Managers became Tat On Shipping & Enterprises Co Ltd. 1995 : Managers became Qingdao Ocean Shipping Company (COSCO QINGDAO), Qingdao/Tsingtao, People's Republic of China. 2001 : Managers became Cosbulk Carrier Co Ltd (COSBULK), Tianjin, People's Republic of China. 2002 : Sold to Winlight Shipping Inc Cosbulk Carrier Co Ltd (COSBULK), Tianjin, People's Republic of China, managers). Transferred to Panama flag.

VESSELS MANAGED ON BEHALF OF FEDNAV LIMITED, MONTREAL, BY HUDSON STEAMHIP CO LTD.

Fe.1 **Thekwini** 1992 - 1993

O.N. 632750   14741g 7329n 15175d   193,20m x 27,06m x 9,106m
2 x 9-cylinder 4SA MAN oil engines, each single reduction geared to a screw shaft by Kawasaki Heavy Industries Ltd, Kobe, Japan

31.3.1977 : Launched by Sasebo Heavy Industries Co Ltd, Sasebo, Japan, (Yard No 256) for Deutsche Dampfschiffahrts-Gesellschaft 'Hansa', West Germany, as **Rabenfels**. 7.1977 : Completed. 1981 : Sold to Lykes Bros Steamships Co Inc, New Orleans, USA, and renamed **Cygnus** for charter to the United States Military Sealift Command. 1990 : Sold to ASL Atlantic Searoute Ltd, (Fednav Ltd, Halifax, Nova Scotia, managers), and renamed **ASL Cygnus** and transferred to the Bahamas register. 1991 : Owners became Cygnus Ltd Partnership, (ASL Atlantic Searoute Ltd, Montreal, managers). 1992 : Managers became Hudson Steamship Co Ltd, Brighton, and renamed **Thekwini**. 1993 : Sold to the Government of United States of America (Department of Transportation), USA, and renamed **Cape Taylor**. 1995 : Managers became Stapp Towing Co Inc, Dickinson, Texas. 1996 : Owners became Government of The United States of America (Transportation Department, Maritime Administration [MarAd]), USA. 1997 : Deleted from *Lloyd's Register* following transfer to the US Naval Reserve Fleet.

Thekwini in the Queen Elizabeth Drydock at Falmouth on 13 March 1993.

(Ian Thomson)

Fe.2 **Federal Skeena**   1995

O.N. 16160   As built :   75733g   56783n   140,194d   265,00m   x   43,06m   x   16,801m
                    After 1985 :   83874g   55600n   164,891d   289,01m (inc BB) x 43,06m x 17,422m
6-cylinder 2SA B & W oil engine by Cockerill-Sambre S. A., Seraing, Belgium.

24.11.1982 : Launched by N.V. Scheepswerven, Hoboken, Belgium, (Yard No 899) for Belcan N.V., Belgium, (N.V. UBEM S. A., Antwerp, managers), as **Federal Skeena**. 2.1983 : Completed. 8.11.1985 : Arrived at Antwerp for lengthening by N.V. Boelwerf S. A. 1988 : Owners became Belcan S. A., (UBEM S. A., Antwerp, managers). 1991 : Owners became UBEM S. A., Luxembourg. 1992 : Sold to Fednav (Luxembourg) S. A. , Luxembourg (UBEM S. A., Antwerp, managers). 4.1995 : Managers became Hudson Steamship Co Ltd, Brighton. 5.1995 : Sold to Arte Shipping Co (Louis Dreyfus Armateurs SNC, Paris, managers), and renamed **La Cordillera** (Panama flag). 2000 : Sold to Iridum SA, and renamed **Christopher** (Cyprus flag). 2000 : Managers became Transmed Shpg S A, Athens. 22.12.01 : When on a voyage from Puerto Bolivar to the Tees with coal, she reported that her engine had stopped and one bow hatch was open and taking in water in heavy weather. An oil slick was located by Coast Guards the following day in position 41.02N, 29.19W off Graciosa Island in the Azores and lifeboats were found on 25.12.2001. She was presumed to have sunk with the loss of her 27 crew and further searches were abandoned.

Federal Skeena   (Company archives)

Fe.3 *Federal Hunter*   1995

O.N. 16174   As built :   75733g 56783n 140,194d   256,01m x 43,06m x 16,801m
               After 1985 :   83874g 55600n 164,891d   289,01m (inc BB) x 43,06m x 17,422m
6-cylinder 2SA B&W oil engine by Cockerill-Sambre SA, Seraing, Belgium.

1.3.1984 : Launched by N.V. Boelwerf S. A., Hoboken, Belgium, (Yard No 900) for N.V. Belcan, Belgium (N.V. UBEM S. A., Antwerp, managers) as *Federal Hunter*. 6.1984 : Completed. 16.8.1985: Arrived at Antwerp for lengthening by N.V.Boelwerf S. A. 1988 : Owners became Belcan S. A., Belgium (UBEM S. A., Antwerp, managers). 1991 : Owners became UBEM S. A., Luxembourg. 1992 : Sold to Fednav (Luxembourg) S. A., Luxembourg (UBEM S A, Antwerp, managers). 4.1995 : Managers became Hudson Steamship Co Ltd, Brighton. 6.1995 : Sold to Oltramare Shipping Co, (Louis Dreyfus Armateurs SNC, Paris, managers); transferred to Panama flag. 1995 : Sold to Setal Denizcilik AS, (Semih Sohtorik Deniz Islemeciligi ve Agentelik AS [Semih Sohtorik Management & Agency Inc], Istanbul, managers) and renamed *Marine Hunter*. 2001 : Sold to Sunshine Shipping Ltd, (Semih Sohtorik Deniz Islemeciligi ve Agentelik AS [Semih Sohtorik Management & Agency Inc], Istanbul, managers); transferred to Marshall Islands flag.

Federal Hunter (Company archives)

VESSELS MANAGED ON BEHALF OF COMPANIES OWNED BY ARMEMENT MARSEILLE-FRET SA, MARSEILLE, FRANCE, BY HUDSON STEAMSHIP CO LTD

Ma.1 *Evening Star* / *CGM Saint-Georges*   1992 - 1993

O.N. 708881   10179g   5517n   15922d   154,24m (inc BB) x 22,89m x 9,051m
5-cylinder 4SA oil engine, single reduction geared to a screw shaft, by Grandi Motori Trieste, Trieste, Italy

27.7.1979 : Launched by Italcantieri SpA, Monfalcone, Italy, (Yard No 4366), as part of a four-ship contract for Traghetti del Mediterraneo SpA, Italy, as *Transbaltico*. While fitting out, all four ships were taken over by the builder after the owners went bankrupt and were laid up pending sale. 7.1981 : Completed for P T Perusahaan Pelayaran Samudera 'Gesuri Lloyd', Jakarta, Indonesia, as *Ganda Bhakti*. 1988 : Sold to Fabulous Shipping Corp, (Perseus Shipping Co Ltd, Tokyo, managers), and renamed *Bright Singapore* (Panama flag). 1988 : Owners became Fabulous Shipping Corp, (Perseus Shipping Co Ltd, Tokyo, managers), and renamed *Transroll* (Philippines flag). 1989 : Sold to Morena Shipping Co Ltd, (Columbia Ship Management Ltd, Limassol, managers), and renamed *Evening Star* (Cyprus flag). 1992 : Managers became Hudson Steamship Co Ltd, Brighton. 1993 : Renamed *CGM Saint-Georges*. 1993 : Managers became Compagnie Maritime Marfret, Marseilles. 1995 : Sold to Sea Harbour Shipping Ltd, (Bogazzi Servizi Navali SrL, Avenza, managers), and renamed *Bandama Express* (St Vincent & the Grenadines flag). 1995 : Renamed *Ville D'Abidjan*. 1995 : Renamed *Sea Lion*. 1999 : Sold to Alarmbay Shipping Co Ltd, (Gripsholm Shipping S.A., Piraeus, managers), and renamed *Lotus* (Cyprus flag). 21.10.1999 : Laid up at Corunna. 2000 : Sold to Indian shipbreakers. 30.4.2000 : Sailed Corunna for Alang in tow of *Dea Captain*. 12.8.2000 : arrived at Alang for demolition.

Evening Star photographed
on 28 October 1989.

(Hans Tiedemann)

Guyane

(Author's collection)

Ma.2 *Guyane* 1992 - 1993

O.N. 708655   15499g 4649n 15922d   154,24m (inc BB) x 22,89m x 9,051m
5-cylinder 4SA oil engine, single reduction geared to a screw shaft, by Grandi Motori Trieste, Trieste, Italy. 1996 : re-engined with 8-cylinder 4SA MaK engine by Krupp MaK Maschinenbau GmbH, Kiel, West Germany

27.7.1979 : Launched by Italcantieri SpA, Monfalcone, Italy, (Yard No 4365) as part of a four-ship contract for Traghetti del Mediterraneo SpA, Italy, as *Transpacifico*. While fitting out all four ships were taken over by the builder after the owner went bankrupt and were laid up pending sale. 7.1981 : Completed for P T Perusahaan Pelayaran Samudera 'Gesuri Lloyd', Jakarta, Indonesia, as *Ganda Gama*. 1988 : Sold to unidentified Panama-flag owners believed to be associated with Perseus Shipping Co Ltd, Tokyo, and renamed *Bright Amsterdam*. 1988 : Sold to Blue Shire Marine Ltd, (Columbia Ship Management Ltd, Limassol, managers), and renamed *Guyane* (Cyprus flag). 1992 : Managers became Hudson Steamship Co Ltd, Brighton. 1993 : Managers became Compagnie Maritime Marfret, Marseilles. 1994 : Owners became Compagnie Maritiime Marfret, Marseilles, France, renamed *Taabo* and transferred to the St Vincent & Grenadines register. 1995 : Renamed *Guyane*. 1999 : Renamed *Nordana Express*. 1999 : Owners became Blue Shire Marine Co Ltd, (Compagnie Maritime Marfret, Marseilles, managers), and renamed *Guyane*. 2001 : Sold to North Coast Shipping Corp, (Gulf Liner Shipping Angencies, Dubai, managers), and renamed *Global Paramount*. 2004 : Sold to Ducky Sovereign Shipping S. A. (TMT Co Ltd, Taipei, Taiwan). Renamed *Ducky Splendid* (Panama flag).

Ma.3 *Saint Pierre* 1992 - 1993

O.N. 705414   9239g 5197n 12091d   145,88m (inc BB) x 21,59m x 8,440m
6-cylinder 2SA Sulzer oil engine by H Cegielski, Poznan, Poland.

7.9.1979 : Launched for H. Schuldt, Hamburg, by Stocznia Szczecinska im A Warskiego, Szczecin, Poland, (Yard No B430/11). 1979 : Sold while fitting out to Midland Montague Leasing (UK) Ltd (Elder Dempster Lines Ltd, Liverpool, managers), and renamed *Sapele*. 1.1980 : Completed. 1987 : Sold to COMARIN S. A. (Marseille Fret SA, Marseilles, later Armement Marseille-Fret S. A., Marseilles, managers), and renamed *Antilles*. 1990 : Managers became Compagnie Maritime Marfret, Marseilles. 1990 : Sold to Lamyra Marine Co Ltd, (Columbia Shipmanagement Ltd, Limassol, managers), and renamed *Saint Pierre* (Cyprus flag). 1992 : Managers became Hudson Steamship Co Ltd, Brighton. 1993 : Managers became Compagnie Maritime Marfret, Marseilles. 1996 : Transferred to the St Vincent & Grenadines register. 1997 : Sold to Seatrano Shipping Co Ltd, (Astra Maritime Inc, Athens, managers). 1998 : Renamed *Astra Sea* (Cyprus flag).

The **Saint Pierre** was photographed at Fort de France, Martinique, in July 1992.

(Author's collection)

VESSELS TECHNICALLY MANAGED ON BEHALF OF PETER DOHLE BY MIDOCEAN TECHNICAL SERVICES LTD

Do.1 **Patricia**   1990 - 1991
O.N. 15830   6871g 4505n 10424d   127,18m (inc.BB.) x 19,92m x 8,302m
6-cylinder 4SA oil engine single reduction geared to a screw shaft by Krupp MaK Maschinebau GmbH, Kiel, West Germany

19.5.1983 : Launched by Schlichting-Werft GmbH, Travemünde, West Germany, (Yard No 1463) for Helmut Bastian Reederei m.s. "Fulmarus" KG, (Helmut Bastian, later Helmut Bastian Reederei, Bremen, managers), as **Fulmarus**. 5.1983 : Completed as **Contract Pioneer**. 1986 : Renamed **Fulmarus**. 1986 : Renamed **Taabo**. 1989 : Sold to Peter Dohle Schiffahrts K.G. (GmbH) & Co, Hamburg. 1990 : Managers became Navigo Management Co, Limassol, and transferred to the Cypriot register. 1990 : Renamed **Medipas Bay**. 1990 : Owners became Partenreederei m/s "Patricia", (Midocean Maritime Ltd, Isle of Man, managers [technical managers Midocean Technical Services Ltd]), and renamed **Patricia**. 1991 : Managers became Peter Dohle Schiffahrts-K.G. GmbH) & Co, Hamburg. 1992 : Renamed **Nedlloyd Formosa**. 1993 : Renamed **Mild Star**. 1994 : Sold to Ashton Associates Inc, (Sunscot & Co Ltd, Hong Kong, managers); transferred to Panama flag. 1994 : Managers became Fleet Trans International Co Ltd, Hong Kong.

The **Patricia** is seen under her original name of **Contract Pioneer**.

(Author's collection)

TECHNICAL MANAGEMENT OF VESSELS CARRIED OUT ON BEHALF OF STOLIDI SHIPPING CO, VALLETTA, MALTA, BY HUDSON STEAMSHIP CO LTD

St.1 **Stolidi**   1993

O.N.   138,764g 106,689n 267,038d   344,43m (inc BB) x 51,90m x 20,767m
Two steam turbines, double reduction geared to a single shaft by Kawasaki Heavy Industry Ltd, Kobe, Japan.

1975 : Ordered by Northern Shipping Inc, Liberia, who refused delivery prior to her launch. 25.1.1976 : Launched by Hyundai Shipbuilding & Heavy Industry Ltd, Ulsan, South Korea, (Yard No 7310) for Asia Merchant Marine Co Ltd, Ulsan, South Korea, a subsidiary company of the builder, as **Korea Banner**. 12.1976 : Completed. 1984 : Owners became Hyundai Merchant Marine Co Ltd, Seoul, South Korea. 1991 : Transferred to the Panamanian register. 1992 : Owners became Inter-play S. A., (Hyundai Merchant Marine Co Ltd, Seoul); transferred to Panama flag. 1993 : Sold to Stolidi Shipping Co Ltd, (Silver Carriers S.A., Piraeus, managers, [technical managers Hudson Steamship Co Ltd, Brighton until 12.1993]) and renamed **Stolidi**; transferred to Malta flag. 20.3.1994 : While on passage from Mina al Fahal to Yosu, South Korea, suffered a flash fire in her accommodation block in a position 19.44N, 63.36E. Her superstructure was gutted and twenty of her crew killed. 22.3.94 : Arrived Umm al Qaiwain anchorage in tow for transhipment of cargo. 7.1994 : Sold to Pakistan shipbreakers. 28.8.1994 : Arrived Gadani Beach for demolition.

INDEX OF HUDSON VESSELS' NAMES

The first column names owned or managed vessels in CAPITAL LETTERS;
the second column gives the fleet list number in *italics*; finally come the page numbers.

Name	Code	Refs	Name	Code	Refs	Name	Code	Refs
Korea Banner	St.1	94	Nafto Cement VI	Th.5	77	SIR ALEXANDER GLEN		
Kota Selamat	Mo.3	84	Napier Star	Mo.6	45,86		Th.4	34,35,38,39, 41,42,77
Kriti Ambassador	Mo.2	83	Nedlloyd Formosa	Do.1	94	Skopelos	JH.2	67
Kurzeme	MT.1	81	Nicholaos Angelakis	Mo.9	88	Slemish	9	60
La Cordillera	Fe.2	53,91	Nikitos K	5	59	Sonia 1	22	39,51,66
La Villa	MT.2	15,82	Nordana Express	Ma.2	93	Spinanger	JH.2	24,67
LANDGUARD POINT			Norgas Traveller	Th.3	76	St Edmund	MT.3	82
	Ca.2	38,39,81	Obelix	Mo.2	83	St Tobias	JH.5	69
Leal	JH.1	67	Ocean Mandarin	Th.4	42,77	STOLIDI	St.1	52,94
Lisbet Terkol	Ca.1	37,80	Ocean Monarch	Th.4	77	Sumava	Mo.13	90
LOLWORTH	6	5,8,59	Oelfine Gas	Th.3	76	Taabo (1977)	Mo.6	86
Lotus	Ma.1	92	Orangeleaf	JH.6	30,70	Taabo (1979)	Ma.2	93
Lugano	18	65	OSTFRIESLAND	Mo.3	42,43,84	Taabo (1983)	Do.1	94
Lung Meng	Ma.7	86	OXSHOTT	1	5,710,11,58	THEKWINI	Fe.1	44,45,52,90, 91
Lux Freeway	Th.8	79	PATRICIA	Do.1	43,94			
MACBRAE	10	10,11,14,61	Pelineon	JH..2	67	Theodosia V	JH.2	67
Mattheos L	Mo.9	88	PHILIPP M	11	11,61	Toplou Bay	JH.2	67
Marine Hunter	Fe.3	53,92	Pigassos	Th.6	78	Transbaltico	Ma.1	92
Maritime Fortune	Mo.11	89	Polly	12	61	Transpacifico	Ma.2	93
Medipas Bay	Do.1	94	Porto Nova	JH.4	68	Transroll	Ma.1	92
MIERVALDIS	MT.3	11,82	Possehl	Mo.10	88	Trilight	Mo.2	83
Mild Star	Do.1	94	Puerto De Aguilas	Th.5	77	Tyba	Du.4	73
MISHREF	Du.2	33,34,73	Rabenfels	Fe.1	90	UPMINSTER (1)	3	5,6,58
Monge	Du.3	73	Rallia	Mo.6	86	UPMINSTER (2)	7	6,7,8,60
MOS FREEWAY	Th.8	42,79	Red Sea	Th.2	36,75	Ushuaia	Mo.8	87
MOSBAY	Mo.4	41,44,85	Roll Vigo	Th.8	79	Vaimama	Mo.8	87
MOSCLIFF	Th.9	45,52,53,79, 80	Rosella	19	65	Valka	MT.1	81
MOSDALE	Mo.13	44,90	S. A. Ostfriesland	Mo.3	84	Van Enterprise	Mo.4	85
MOSDEEP	Th.7	42,44,45,52, 53,78,79	Saga	14	63	VARANGFJELL	TC.1	27,34,35,74
MOSGULF	Mo.10	42,44,45,88	SAINT PIERRE	Ma.3	45,93,94	Vedalin	19	65
MOSHILL	Mo.14	44,90	Sainte Suzanne	Mo.7	86	VILK	MT.2	10,11,15,17, 82
MOSLAKE	Mo.12	42,45,89	San Roberto	21	66			
MOSRIVER	Mo.11	42,45,52,89	Sanaga	Mo.4	85	Ville D'Abidjan	Ma.1	92
MOSSTAR	Th.6	41,43,78	Sapele	Ma.3	93	Vulcan	Mo.1	83
MOSTANK	Mo.2	41,43,83,84	Saqr Yanbu	Mo.11	89	War Boyne	6	5,59
MOSTWEEN 2	Mo.1	41,43,83	SCT Vincent	Mo.7	86	War Browny	4	5,58,59
MOSTWEEN 4	Mo.5	42,44,85	Sea Ilex	Mo.13	90	War Ness	5	5,59
MOSTWEEN 5	Mo.6	42,45,52,86	Sea Lion	Ma.1	92	WARDEN POINT	Th.2	36,37-41,43, 47,75,76
MOSTWEEN 6	Mo.7	42,44,50,86, 87	Sea Magnolia	Mo.14	90			
MOSTWEEN 7	Mo.9	42,44,45,52, 53,88	Seakap	Ca.2	81	Welda	Mo.10	88
			Selda	Mo.4	85	Westralia	JH.7	30,49,70
MOSTWEEN 8	Mo.8	42,44,87	Serene	JH.1	67	X-Press Annapurna	Mo.3	84
Mrs B	Ca.2	39,81	Shane	22	66	Xingda	Mo.12	89
Mt Powell	Mo.5	85	Silver Gulf	Mo.8	87	Yamaoki Maru	Th.7	78,79
Mytilini	Ca.1	80	Silverness	Mo.6	86	Yong Shun	Mo.1	83
			Sincerogas	Du.3	73	Zetta	Mo.10	88
			Siona	MT.1	81			
			Sir Alexander	Th.4	42,77			